Nourish

A journey to loving and embracing the woman within

Krystle J Bailey

enjoy the journey!

Krystle J Bailey
xo!

Published by Live Your Truth, LLC 2017.

Dedication

To Elliana: My world was forever changed the day you came into my life. You did more than make me a mommy; you made me a better me. You continue to inspire me to new heights every day of your life. No matter where life takes you, know that I am always in your corner cheering you on.

To Maceo: My strong and gentle monster. You taught me a new kind of love——that between a mother and son. You filled me up in a way that I didn't know I needed. You'll conquer the world one day with that smile and I will always be your home base.

To Nick: Your undying belief in me is the wind beneath my wings. You are my back bone, my strength, my rock. It is my honor to be your partner in life.

Table of Contents

Introduction

I am a dreamer. Often a dreamer and not a doer. I've dreamt all my life about writing a book one day. I wrote books about cats and dogs as a child. I'd grab five or six sheets of printer paper from my mother's desk, write a story of hope and love, rainbows and sunshine. Then I'd staple it at the top left corner and write proudly across the front, "Written and Illustrated by Krystle Bailey." My mom and my uncle still hold on to a few of my books. Every time I wrote one, I would feel an exhilarating rush of pride when I handed it to my mom. I had written something just for her, courtesy of my young imagination and wild heart.

I was an overweight kid. I struggled with insecurities and doubts of what I would ever be good at. I played softball for many years but my love of food always kept me heavier and slower than my friends. I never aspired to be a famous softball player one day or any kind of athlete for that matter.

We moved when I was in fourth grade, just when students were asked which instruments we wanted to play at my old school. I wanted to play the clarinet; maybe that would be what I would be good at one day. The clarinet sounded fun. It was art and I loved to create. We were moving though so I pushed the thought aside and figured if I had the opportunity in my new school, that I would learn the clarinet.

Moving to a new town is a challenge. Moving to a new town as the *big girl* is double the work. My personality had to shine big time or I would risk being left out, or worse—bullied. So my focus became being good at being me. I was a good friend, I was a good listener, my mom was totally the cool mom, I was silly

2

and outgoing. I was great at being me but that took a whole lot of energy because the way I saw it, if my personality was big enough, people wouldn't be able to see how big my body was. I could hide behind my smile, my giving and nurturing personality, and my silliness.

Better yet, I was smart and being smart was great for the boys who didn't want to study for their tests. I'd just get all my test answers right and strategically move my arm so they could see the answers. Sitting next to me was a wonderful place to be if you didn't want to study for the Friday math test.

I never did pick up the clarinet though. Softball became my activity of choice a few years later. Softball was fun because playing first base needed a bigger, stockier person to hold it down and while I was slow, I was strong so I could hit well. I played softball for a few years and eventually gave it up when running several miles for practice became part of the deal.

I also gave up being smart when being smart wasn't cool anymore—when being smart meant being a geek. I couldn't be a geek *and* the big girl so I had to adapt to the changes of life in grade school. That's what I was good at—adapting when it was needed. Adjusting so that I would always be accepted. I would just change how I did this, or learn how to do that. I'd find a way to make sure I had *something* to keep me important to the other kids and as long as I had *something*, maybe they would never notice that I was on the heavier side.

Writing though. Writing was mine. Writing was something that I could do and the only person who had to think I was awesome was me. Writing became my outlet in this season of my life and in every season that followed. When times were good, I wrote. When times were bad, I wrote. I wish I had seen the value in keeping old journals around when I was younger. There must be countless water bottles made from recycled Krystle Bailey journals—the ones I tossed when I thought that season of my life didn't matter anymore. If only I knew then what I know now about the little treasures of life. Writing was a constant and something that nobody could take from me. It was something that I didn't have to force, I didn't have to answer to anyone about, and I didn't have to share unless I wanted to. It was my freedom.

Writing became a back-burner *hobby* as I entered my high school and college years. I would write occasionally in a journal or knock out a new poem every couple of months but it was just that—a hobby. Being valuable and important in high school was a whole new ball game, one we will get into later in the book. The energy that I needed to spend to be seen as more than *the big girl,* when at that point, I was well over 200 pounds, took way more out of me than I had to give.

I battled with hidden depression often during high school. I spent a lot of time giving my body away for attention. I did, however, also spend a lot of positive energy in calligraphy class experimenting with different forms of art. Mrs. Reustle loved me and I was accepted in that room in so many ways. I would skip my lunch room hour to spend it in the art room, creating. As long as I was creating, I was happy. I might not be Van Gogh but I was okay with that. Creating gave me joy and a finished art project breathed life into me. That said, I was average at best.

I longed to be great at something and what I was actually great at was collecting dust in my bedroom while I was out there trying to figure out what I could be good at. When I was in college, I met

Nick, my now-husband. I quickly got pregnant with my daughter, Elliana. This I knew I could be great at. I knew for sure that I could be a great mother and a great wife because Nick was going to marry me right away. I was pregnant, and that was the thing to do, right? Not in Nick's world. We are marrying this year right before the publishing of this book, eight years later.

Understanding Nick and where I fit into his life, figuring out pregnancy and becoming a new mom, the loss of my father that same year, and life as an adult posed way more challenges than figuring out how to be important in the fifth grade. So, I did what I do best when under pressure. I bought a new notebook and I began to write.

Fast forward a few years and my writing entered a new stage. After Elliana was born, I began a journey to weight loss that would begin to shape my story as it is today. In the process, I began to share my day by day on social media, which eventually led to a blog—*Skinny Jeans Dreams.* I shared authentically, from the heart, and through it all. I shared the good, the bad, and the ugly. Well, most of the ugly. I still kept a journal for the ugliest of times, which you'll read in the coming chapter. I wrote about my weigh-in days, my fitness, my struggles, my victories, my daughter, my traveling. I wrote about it all. In the process, I was asked constantly, "When will you write a book? To which my response was always, *I don't know. One day.*

I was terrified of writing a book for the public. My writing has always been my own. My blogs were for fun and my journals were my getaway. A book? That would be new territory I was not sure I was ready for. What if nobody reads it? What if it fails? What if someone *gasp* criticizes me? Better yet, what if this weight loss doesn't last and I am seen as a fraud? It just wasn't the time and I wasn't sure it ever would be but I continued to answer with *one day.*

I know now, in retrospect, that my story wasn't done unfolding. My story is not one only of weight loss. Yes, weight loss (and gain) are a piece of my story but that's it—just a piece. That part of my life was a stepping stone to learning who Krystle really is. It shed layers not just physically but opened the door to shedding personal, mental, and emotional layers so that I could get to the core of who I am. I was shocked to find what I found at that core.

I found that I , really, kind of, like myself. No, I love myself. And it has nothing to do with my weight, my body image, how smart I am, or how much I do for other people to make them like me. With all the layers stripped away, I learned to love me for me. Just because I *am.*

Introduction

I am Krystle J Bailey. It took me a long time to learn what that really meant. The stories in this book are valuable and important shaping forces that molded me to be who I am today. I pray that this book will bring you hope, moments of self-reflection, encouragement, and most of all—the invitation to seek out who you truly are, beyond all the layers, beyond the scars, beyond the facade. Who you are is so beautiful and when you connect with her, that, my friend, is where life truly begins. Let's dig in.

Don't try to fix me, I'm not broken.

I don't need a cream or a cleanse to undo the marks of my journey.

I don't need a quick fix or magic for me to love who I am with certainty.

Don't try to fix me, I'm not broken.

I don't need to shrink my hips or fill my lips, I don't need injections or suctions from my midsection, I don't need their interjection for me to love my reflection.

Don't try to fix me, I'm not broken.

I don't need to shrink it, fill it, tuck it, dye it, lengthen it, cover it, fake it, or shake it for me to feel...

Beautiful.

I don't need to give back the souvenirs of a life well traveled because the media tells me lies

Like: "A changing body is only good if it's shrinking"

Like: "Moms shouldn't look like they're actually moms"

Introduction

Like: "Grey hair is a bad thing"

Like: "Smile lines must be filled in"

Like: "THIS body isn't already beach worthy"

Don't try to fix me, I'm not broken.

And neither are you.

Truth bombs in 3 ... tick, tick, boom:

Your smile shows your character,

Your laugh lights up a room,

Your body is a wonderland,

Your presence sings a beautiful tune,

Your story is uniquely your own,

Your scars are marks of victory,

There is no shame in letting them be shown,

Your voice is important,

Allow it to be spoken,

You don't need to be fixed.

You are not broken.

By Krystle J Bailey 2017

Nourishment

Nourish. That word refreshes my soul. There are certain words that fill me up in a way that feels like a cold glass of water on a sweltering summer day. Nourish or nourishment. These words give me that same satisfaction and contentment when I hear them.

For the last several years, my vision board has included: *Write the book.* With every passing year, I have failed to even start the book. Deep down, hidden in my heart, I knew the time was coming but I could not seem to bring it to life. The months would pass and I would continue to tell myself that when the time was right, I would write. Decembers continued to come and go again, and I would just be faced with another January and a new vision board. Again, I'd write out my personal, business, and family goals and include: *Write the book.*

For years this went on until this one. Every year, I read the book *One Word That Will Change Your Life* by Jon Gordon. The concept of the book is living your year in accordance with one specific word given to you by God, the universe, or whomever or whatever it is that feeds your spirit. For me, that's God. In years past, my words have been "be", "pray", "connect" and these words have changed the course of that year drastically. This year, my word is "finish". I can now see how my first three words have set the stage for this year's word. My word, "finish" came to me early in December of last year when I was visualizing what I needed to change in my life to take myself to the next level. I wanted to become whatever it was that God needed me to be and frankly, I was tired of feeling so average at everything I set out to do. I knew there was something out there for me. I could feel it in the depths of my heart but fear, doubt, and insecurities would never allow it to come to life. That is, without prayer, connection, and learning how to just be in the moment.

The word "finish" rang over and over in my mind until one day, I was reading my morning devotionals and I asked the Lord to show me clearly what my word for this upcoming year should be. As I normally do, I doubted whether the word that I was hearing was the word that I needed. Was it my own mind making this up or was it the universe or the Holy Spirit? So, I asked God to identify my word in His word. *Just make it clear cut for me for once in my life, God, puh-lease! In Jesus' name. Did I say please?*

That morning, as I read the Bible, I read about Nehemiah and his rebuilding of the walls of Jerusalem against adversity and criticism. It was a short devotional excerpt and it was all that I needed. In the

15

scripture, I read the words, "it is finished." On the most spiritual level, I knew that God was calling me to live out my purpose. I knew that I had been letting life, distraction, fear of criticism, and adversity block me from my purpose. It was time to finish what God needed me to finish in ways that I expected and, I am learning, in ways that I haven't. It was time to finally write and publish that book.

In addition to the word of the year, I have a few core words that ring over and over in my mind and as the seasons of my life change, those words change. In this season, some of those words include "intentional", "legacy", "love", and my most recent word: nourish.

Nourish was given to me when I was staring at myself in the mirror one morning asking God to help me continue my journey of health in a way that provides wellbeing for my mind. I asked Him to show me how to continue so that I could sustain a healthy

16

lifestyle forever. I was tired of dieting and tired of feeling like if I wasn't on a nutritional *plan* then I was doing something wrong. I was seeking more out of life in every way. The word "nourish" came out of my mouth that day as I eyed my body up and down. Nourish. Nourish your body, your mind, your spirit, your relationships, your life. The word that refreshed my spirit was the word that would change everything. Nourish, oh it's so sweet. I repeated it over and over and as it rang through my lips and built a billboard between my two ears, I knew it was the tiny little piece that I had been missing. It was the piece that would bring to life my book.

If there is one thing I am working to improve, it's trusting my intuition the first time. I haven't mastered the whole intuition thing just yet, so I had to look deeper to make sure of what I already knew. I began to look back on what my message had been on social media recently. Sharing my heart, thoughts, words, and inspiration began in 2011 when I started to share the weight loss journey that I was traveling openly on social media—initially through a blog and then onto the world of Facebook, Instagram, Twitter, etc.

As I evolved, my message evolved. For almost six years, I have been sharing publicly in an effort to inspire others in a positive way. It started with weight loss and has evolved to become a wide variety of topics that I offer insight, reflection, or experience on. As the seasons of my life change, my message changes. As I grow, my message grows.

As I reflected on the message I had been bringing to the public in this season of my life through social media and in my conversations, I could see clearly that my message had unintentionally been to nourish our lives in every capacity. My message to other women that I had been sharing from the heart for months was right there in front of me, packed into a perfect little word with a bow just waiting for me to unwrap it and do with it what my soul desired: Write. So here we are.

We all just want to live well. Isn't that the overall goal? Our heart's truest desires are not to be a certain weight, make a certain amount of money, or hold a certain title. At the core of who we are, we want to feel at peace, important, and content. I've searched the world for that contentment only to find that the only place to truly find it is within my heart. It was already here, waiting for me to discover it. There is a peace that washes over you when you find that what you've been looking for, you already have within you. Now that I've found it, my job is to take care of it—to nourish it and to help you to do the same.

What does it mean to nourish? To many, when they hear the word *nourish*, they think of food and physical nourishment while others relate the word to spiritual nourishment. Nourishment can mean different things to different people. How nourishment graces my life may look a little bit different for you and that is okay. I want it to look different. My goal is to help you to understand and identify what makes you feel whole, well, and at peace and then to encourage you to pursue that in a way that satisfies your soul. For me, nourishment means taking care of my four main priorities. These are my four cornerstones for living a well-balanced life and I want to pass them along to you. Yours may be the same or slightly different and that is absolutely encouraged.

As in all areas of self-improvement, I always say to take what is meant for you here and leave the rest. Every book you read, every conversation you have, every speaker you hear should be absorbed in the same way. Not everything that every inspirational person says is meant for your life specifically. Take each moment for what it is, apply to your life in a way that makes sense to you, leave the rest, and move on to what's next.

If you were living exactly like me, you wouldn't be authentically you. If I were living exactly like my favorite author or speaker, I wouldn't be authentically who I am. Everything that I know and write about is learned and experienced from other sources, mixed together with my own life experiences, and repackaged to fit my life. I encourage you to do the same. Repackage all that you learn and all that speaks to your heart and mind in a way that makes sense for your personal life.

My four key areas of nourishment are:

- Spirit

- Mind

- Body

- Relationships

When these four areas work together in balance and are well fed is when I feel the most whole. Let's take a look at what it means to nourish. For this context, my favorite of the Merriam-Webster definitions of the word *nourish* is, "to cause (something) to develop or grow stronger." My desire is to develop these four areas of my life to their fullest potential so that my cup is overflowing in every area. My prayer is that I am always observant enough and self-reflective enough to know when one or more areas need a little more tender loving care so that my circle is always full.

Have you ever looked at a restaurant menu, seeking what you want for lunch and unable to decide so you start by crossing out what you know that you don't want? That's how I pretty much always order food. And then I order something completely off the wall but that's another story. In the same *process of elimination* fashion, when I know I am pursuing something for my life, I find it important to identify the opposite or what I know I don't want to order for my life.

We identified what it means to nourish but what is the opposite of nourish? Antonyms include, to discourage, frustrate, hinder, or inhibit. I don't know about you but I am good without any of those words being a part of my life! As a matter of fact, I safeguard myself from experiencing those feelings to the best of my ability.

When you are clearly defining what you want in life, it is just as important to clearly identify what you do not. Identifying the feelings or experiences that you don't want to have will also help you to identify the people, conversations, or situations that trigger those feelings. When you do so, that is the first step in protecting your peace.

Protecting your peace is an inside job. Nobody will do this for you.

I am positive that you are loved and people adore you but nobody (except God) loves you enough to protect your peace for you. That's up to you. Only you know the things that cause turmoil in your heart, mind, and spirit. Once you identify those things, it's your job to safeguard yourself in a loving and protective way.

Take a walk with me, if you will, as I explain how I visualize my personal wellbeing. If my wellbeing or my overall *self* is represented by a circle, place the word *Nourishment* on the inside of that circle. On the outside edges of my circle are the things that are important to me to nourish and take care of in order for me to feel the most whole. Around the perimeter of my circle are my four pillars: spirit, mind, body, and relationships. When my circle feels whole, I feel at peace. I feel nourished, taken care of, and content. The word *Nourish* at the center of my self represents the time, energy, effort, and resources that I am adding to my life to make sure that my circle is full. I am making time each day to nourish myself with the things that expand my circle in every direction. When my circle is whole, I feel whole. When my circle is sinking on one corner, starting to look like an oval or a straight line, I know I need to direct energy to one of those areas to push my circle back out to full capacity.

There are a million different things that could be on the outside of this circle that may be important to you. Through years of talking to people, reading books, and listening to speakers, I have gathered that we all have essentially the same core values, give or take a few. Many might include business or career on the outside of their circle, others may want to include ministry or volunteer work, purpose or passions, and so on. The reason that my four are simple is because I know that when these four areas of my life are thriving, I am thriving. When my spirit, mind, body, and relationships are well, I am able to be the best version of myself, which translates into my career, my ministry, and most of all—my purpose. You've heard the phrase, "you can't pour from an empty cup." My circle is my cup and the way I choose to live life is that I overflow my cup so much that it pours into the lives of others; that the goodness, the hope, the positivity, encouragement, and empowerment that flow out of me when my cup is full is poured into everyone I meet in one way or another. When that happens, my purpose is being fulfilled.

I didn't always live this way. It took me a long time to figure it out and to keep it real. I am still figuring it out every day. We're constantly in motion, in a state of becoming. I am always learning more about who I am and what I want out of life. What I know now, I haven't always known, and there is still so much to experience. I'm a woman, a mom, a wife and one of those alone or all three of those things combined usually equate to giving ourselves to everyone around us until we are run dry with nothing left for ourselves. We are taught that moms are burnt out, tired, and sleep deprived. Women wear the weight of the world on their shoulders and must serve their husbands, host their guests, be super mom, keep a tidy house, and now run a business or work full time too. We can and we should because we're women and we roar mightily, right? We can do it all and not break down because we're powerful, right? We're strong and capable of it all because that's how women were created, right?

Wrong. Not at the expense of our personal wellbeing. Not anymore. Women all over the world are beginning to experience life in this new and exhilarating way. We're beginning to drop the weight of the world and carry only what is important to us and only as far as we need to.

As far as I am concerned, I have traded in that life of needing to do it all for one of peace, wellness, and overflowing nourishment. I've traded in the life of putting myself last for a life that allows me to give so much more by putting myself first. I got tired. Really, really tired. When I am tired, burnt out, and empty, I am serving the least of myself to my husband, our kids, my family, my clients, my friends, and leaving the scraps for God to pick up and put back together.

I didn't want to live like that anymore. Too often, I was finding myself on my bedroom floor crying and overwhelmed, riddled with anxiety and depression because I just did not know how to balance it all, or I'd be calling my husband just because I was sad with no real reason or answer. I didn't know what I needed from him because I just wanted to be sad. I had nothing left in my tank because I had given it all away. I was on the hamster wheel and it sucked. I wanted off.

I don't know what it will take for you to get to that point or maybe you already have and you're already there seeking and longing for a change. Some people will catch it early enough to not have to face the sobbing tears on their bedroom floor while others will spend too long there before they decide to pick back up again. Wherever you are at right now is a beautiful place to be. The important thing is that you're here. You're reading a book with intentions to improve your life in some capacity and that is something to be proud of. You're investing in your life and your personal growth. That is a beautiful thing, my friend. Wherever you are at today, I need you to know that you are enough. Not only are you enough today but you've always been enough. Where you're at today is where you need to be and I, for one, am proud of you.

A little about me and how I got to this place: Nick and I have been together for going on eight years. We have been through it all together including me getting pregnant early in our relationship, to me having to go back to school and finish college with a baby, to moving from apartment to apartment, to living together and hating each other, to having another baby, through the good, the bad, and the ugly. Our relationship is not your average storybook tale. We didn't get married when I got pregnant with our daughter for the sake of getting married. We didn't even know if we would make it but we decided to try for the benefit of Elliana.

I was in college when I was pregnant with her. He was established in his career and is thirteen years older than me. This wasn't at all the plan but we had something worth trying for.

For years we did this dance of passing ships in the night. We would get along most of the time but lacked connection in the early part of our relationship. We would have the occasional date night, many of which ended up in a fight about our future, disrespectful arguments with each other. We went through bouts of being head over heels love when we found ourselves on the same page, followed by me having a breakdown about whether I was wife material. Those were ugly and never ended well. The beginning of our relationship was ugly, it was beautiful, it was all the things in between and it was ours. It's our story and I wouldn't trade it for any other story in the world. When we got engaged after seven years and two kids, my stepmom whispered in my ear as we exchanged champagne toasts: *This is your fairytale, honey.*

Love held us together through it all but I would be lying to tell you it has been easy getting to this place. Our relationship is unique and one of a kind. Nick has always been adamant about people getting married for the right reasons—not because they lived together for a certain number of years, or had kids together, or felt like they should because it was the right thing to do. If Nick was sure of one thing, it was that people should get married because they truly vowed to spend every day of the rest of their life together and life without each other simply did not make sense.

So, for years, Nick and I were boyfriend and girlfriend, living together, and raising children together. To my own fault, mildly out of bitterness, mostly due to being young, and partly because I wanted more from him, I gave him girlfriend effort for many of those years. I did not give him my 100 percent. No, I am not proud to admit this but you need to know this to understand the big picture.

When he asked me to marry him, it triggered a series of changes for the better. After the years of arguments and disagreements regarding marriage, I knew that this was for real. Nick and I were going to spend every day of the rest of our lives together. Maybe it came with age or experience or maybe it was an awakening of sorts but something clicked in me that challenged me to work to bring my best self to the altar. I no longer wanted to give a fraction of myself to my boyfriend. I wanted to give 100 percent of myself—my best self—to my husband.

So began healing, digging deep internally, and exploring what that truly looked like. Add in my years of effort in the department of self-growth, my journey to health, my experience with working with other individuals, mentoring and being mentored, and here I am—content and at peace now with the most authentic and truest version of myself.

It didn't take long to strip down the layers. The dominoes were already set up. I've been reading self-growth books for years. I've been praying for years. I've been self-reflecting for years. The one piece that was missing was the simple desire to strip the layers of the world down so that I could bring my truest, most authentic self, ready to be loved through and through in a new way—by my husband. Put a ring on it and *click* there goes the beautiful display of dominoes toppling that ended with a wedding to plan and a heart to mend.

A desire that strong has the power to peel back even the toughest of onion layers. I don't know what it is for you. Maybe it is something as big as marriage or the simple calling of your soul to live better but whatever it is, I want to share with you my experiences through this journey of healing and nourishment in hopes that you will take away a golden nugget to help you continue your own personal journey of growth.

The chapters that follow are broken down to spell out the word, *nourishment*. These are all lessons I have had to learn, pieces of my story, and stories from inspirational women in my life. These eleven life mantras work together to keep my circle of nourishment full. They are little things that I have picked up along the way that fuel my life and help me to be my personal best.

Before we go, I just want to say that my prayer over this book and every reader is that you will live a little better, pull your shoulders back a little further, and lift your chin a little higher after you've read this book. I pray that you'll always know that you're beautifully and wonderfully made to be exactly who you are. Seeking self-improvement does not mean that you're less than great. It just means that you love yourself enough to get even better and rise a little higher. You're not broken and you don't need to be fixed. You can, however, improve upon what's already beautiful.

N: Nix the Comparison Game

I'm just a girl

Trying to make it in this world

Comparison is the drug of choice

I'm trying to stay sober

I have my own voice

I am not her

She is not me

I am who I am

Strong from within

To be valuable to the world

I don't need to be thin

My truths are my own

My joy is mine alone

My peace is mine to protect

Pieces of it I must recollect

And piece back together

My puzzle of happiness

They told me to do, see, be more

But I just want less

Less noise

Less hustle

Less go go go

They said successful people don't rest

I say no no no

I don't want to be her

I don't want her to be me

I want us both to live authentically

To inspire each other's lives

To help each other to rise

To leave our own legacies

And live our lives with ease

Because we are living our purpose

Free from competition

We no longer feel worthless

We have found our own mission

I'm just a girl

Trying to leave my mark on this world

A girl with a voice

With a story of victory

In which I rejoice
Broken chains of comparison
Are left at my feet
With a voice from deep within
I shout, I am free.
By Krystle J Bailey 2017

As we get ready to dive into several important areas of nourishment and wellbeing, I want to get this out of the way so that you can clear your mind enough to receive and live out what I have to say that follows. Comparison will rob you of all joy in life. Comparing yourself to your fellow sister is pointless and a big waste of energy. We are all doing our best in life and what you see on social media, at mom's club events, or at birthday parties is merely a well-polished highlight reel of everyone's real life.

We all have things that we deal with that are less than admirable. Most people aren't blasting their marriage problems on Facebook, their depression and anxiety on Instagram, or walking into a birthday party shouting about their struggles with food addiction. We are all trying to live our best life and in an age where we are bombarded with images of what *perfect* is supposed to look like. It's easy to find ourselves in the comparison trap. The reality is we all have things that we struggle with, burdens we bear, and secrets that we don't share.

If we stop spending our energy comparing and start spending it by listening and understanding, we will begin to realize how much we all have in common and how if we can band together, we could really make the world a better place. At least the world around us! Every beautiful woman with perfectly filtered picture on your Instagram has problems too and there are twenty other selfies behind that picture that didn't make the cut—ones that didn't make her feel pretty enough, fit enough, or appealing enough to the Instagram eye. Everyone struggles with something and the sooner we can learn to love and embrace each other rather than spend our energy comparing our lives, the sooner we will find ourselves more content and at peace with the life we have been given.

This is your life. If you can take one thing away from this book, I want you to leave knowing that your life is uniquely yours. What is important to you is important because you say so. Who you are is exactly who you were created to be. I am not you and you are not me and that is a beautiful thing! Let's be our most authentic selves together and see how the world can begin to become a better place to live.

As I share stories of my personal life in each of the areas that matter to me, you'll find a recurring theme: Comparison has robbed me of my joy for entirely too long. I have spent too much time doing

41

what the next woman was doing because it seemed like the right thing to do. I've spent too many hours scrolling social media only to look up and find myself in a state of mild depression because I just spent the last hour looking at bodies and lifestyles of other women rather than focusing on my own. I've torn down my body and my mind in a race that I didn't even know I was running but somehow found myself running with a bunch of other women who never signed up either.

I've missed out on my own relationships because I've been so worried about what I could say about it on social media. I've missed months of church because I felt like I wasn't *Christian* enough like the woman next to me who never missed a beat. I've spent holidays upset with my spouse because he didn't get me roses like all the girls on Facebook. The list goes on and on in ways I have wasted precious moments of

42

my life stuck in comparison. As I fully embrace and understand this life of freedom, free from comparison and full of joy, I want to allow you to hear my heart.

I am not perfect at this. I still find myself regularly needing to check my intentions in what I am doing. There is a difference between searching for inspiration and getting trapped in comparison mode and it's a slippery slope. Even as a writer, I find myself needing to set my mind right as I read other books. I read books to enhance my mind, inspire my spirit, and perfect my craft and while it is just as easy to seek inspiration, I will often find myself beginning to compare my writing to hers. It is a natural occurrence and how we are built as women. It's how we have been molded and shaped in a world where comparison is all around us.

In our minds, someone is always doing it better than we can. But it's a vicious and pointless cycle and together we can break it. This is your permission, your invitation to drop out of the race that you never signed up for and begin living at your speed, your way, in the ways that make you feel good inside and out. When we can break this cycle of needing to keep up with each other, we will all be free to live our most genuine, authentic, and beautiful lives just the way they were created for us to live. I can't wait! It's right over the horizon.

O: Open Your Heart and

Mind

Dream with your eyes wide open

Seek the unknown

Go where your fears are broken

Embrace every stepping stone

Take the road less traveled

Live your life out loud

Let your worries unravel

Set them free to the clouds

Open your heart to goodness

Let it flow in

Pursue a life of fullness

Everything you need lies within

By Krystle J Bailey

Let goodness flow in

People often say things to me like, "Awesome stuff always happens to you." or "You're so lucky." While I have experienced some amazing things, I don't consider myself *lucky* at all. I made up in my mind several years ago that I would choose my mindset, my energy, and my outlook on life. Up until that point, nothing good had been happening to me. I didn't have a bad life but I was unhappy with where I was at. I was in college and not at all living the college dream. I knew there could be a better life but it appeared as if everyone around me was living it and I was left in the dark. I was convinced that I was just the unlucky one, the ugly duckling, the black sheep and that it was all the outside things, people, and experiences that were making my life just okay.

One summer, I ran away to Las Vegas. Well, I didn't run away. I was in college and I was unhappy

46

with the direction of my schooling, my love life, my friendships, my living situation and everything else there was to be bitter about, so I decided that Las Vegas would make it better. My aunt and uncle lived out there so I called my aunt one day on a whim, asked if I could come live with her and told her that my dad would pay for my one-way ticket.

I would figure things out when I got there. I didn't know what the plan was but I thought life had to be better on the West Coast. I went out indefinitely with plans to build a new life for myself. I began looking at finishing college out there at University of Nevada, Las Vegas, had my eyes peeled for a guy to date, got a job at Einstein Bagels in hopes of making some new friends, and planted my feet on the dry grounds of the Las Vegas desert.

I learned quickly that not only were my heart and mind the same they were in New Jersey, but that

Las Vegas is the last place to *build a better life* for a single, college kid. Just my humble opinion, no offense to my Vegas friends! The transient lifestyle of a city like Las Vegas was a little too much for my small-town heart to understand and connect with. Everywhere there was fun, there also seemed to be trouble. Trouble was the last thing I needed to build a better life.

The summer passed and I worked, dated a time or two, hung out with my aunt and uncle, lay by the pool, made friends with an older lady who lived in the neighborhood. And by older, I mean I was twenty-one and she was over sixty. My life in Vegas was getting nowhere fast and to no surprise, I was still unhappy. My heart was still bitter from old relationships, life at home didn't seem appealing but I missed my family, and I was still in the *woe is Krystle* mind-frame. The lack of humidity in the desert made my hair awesome

48

so that was a win. Midsummer, after learning that my sister was having a baby boy, I decided to come back home. My nephew would give me something to love and connect to and I just couldn't imagine not being with my sister at this time of her life.

I came home mid-August and I moved in with my grandmother. It was during this time that I was able to spend real time with myself. I had my own room in her house and I didn't want to be a burden on my grandparents so a lot of the time there, I was either commuting to college or in my room where I would journal and reflect. Moving to Vegas wouldn't fix things, moving home wouldn't fix things, so what would allow me to begin living better? I didn't want to stay in this place and I was quickly fading into a depression that I wanted no part of.

At the same time, I met Nick. I was so young and naive, tired of heartbreaks and meaningless relationships. I didn't know where things would go with him and me but I was working on me in the process. I looked back in my journal from this time and it's quite comical reading entries from when you're twenty-one years old and trying to not fall in love.

I got a good laugh out of it but what I also saw was the clear defining moment when I decided that I deserved good. I wrote a piece about how I planned to deal with negative feelings moving forward. I also drew a silly little illustration—I can write; I can *not* draw! The image was of me with little lines of long straggly hair and a pointy nose, eyes that looked sunk into my face, and lips that were too big for my head. Beyond the ridiculous representation of myself, there were also little plus signs with arrows pointing towards my nose representing breathing positive energy in. There were also negative signs and arrows pointing away from my face that came from my mouth,

50

representing breathing negative out. As silly as it seems, and as silly as the rest of the entire journal is in retrospect, this little illustration is something that I still hold on to. I still do this when I meditate or when I am stressed. I envision these plus signs coming in and negative signs going out to bring myself back to calm.

The rest of what I wrote about in that season of my life was a mixture of dates with Nick, leaving my toothbrush at his house, random thoughts like, "Why do couples feel the need to walk with their arms around each other when there is no room to walk?" or "What makes a good thing *good* and a bad thing *bad*? And why do we sometimes refer to things that are good as being *bad?*"

I was figuring out the world around me as a young adult and albeit slightly ridiculous, it was also self-reflective. It was in this season that I decided to stop accepting negative energy and open my heart to all that was good. It was at this time of my life that I decided to experience whatever it was that life had to offer with a positive outlook and a heart that was open to adventure, change, and growth. This was where I began seeking the silver lining and only accepting a glass as half full.

As I reflect back on the years between then and now, I have gone through heartache and tough times like anybody else but I have also experienced so much good and so many blessings. Recently, after I was chosen for an exclusive group to try out a new fitness program before it launched, my friend texted me and said, "There is always cool sh*t happening to you!" My response was that I set myself up for cool stuff to happen to me.

Being someone who experiences cool stuff isn't about luck or good juju, if you ask me. It's about blessings and even more so, it's about being open to receiving those blessings. It's about working hard, showing up, being an open book, and having an open mind. It's about being prepared when opportunity presents itself and bringing your personal best to each situation without any ulterior motive or intent other than to be present in each moment as it is presented.

Experiencing life to the fullest means sometimes you're going to try something and fail at it but you won't know the lesson that's meant for you there until you give it a go. It means that sometimes relationships will fall apart and sometimes your heart will hurt but you'll build character and strength that you will carry with you into the next relationship, as will the other person. It means being open to what people, places, and experiences have to teach you. You don't know everything and you never will. All you know now is what you know so be open to what else there is that you need to learn.

Life lessons abound in everyday life if you're open to them and seeking them out. Opportunity is everywhere if you're open to receive it. Good people, life-shifting conversations, breathtaking views, and life adventures are everywhere every day when your heart and mind are open.

Hindsight is always going to be 20/20 but we won't get to experience hindsight until it's too late to change things so all we can do is bring our best today. I don't know what will happen to my life in another ten or twenty years, or even tomorrow, but I know that it will have purpose. I can't change the past; I can't change the future. All I can do is live with my heart wide open—open to the things that will make me better and know that when I fall, I will always bounce back. God will always heal all wounds even if they leave scars, things will always be okay in the long run, and I will always rise above.

I know it because I claim it to be true. Start today to breathe in the positivity and breathe out the negativity. Each moment of our lives is a steppingstone. I didn't know where my life would take me when I drew my little picture back in 2009. All I knew then was all I knew. I didn't know anything about parenting, marriage, losing a parent, weight loss, fitness, business, real life bills, taking care of a home, or anything that I know now. But all I had at that time was all that I needed to put one foot in front of the other.

Every moment is an opportunity to look forward, to keep your heart open, to seek out what's next for you. Just don't forget to be present in the moment—there are life lessons waiting there for you and experiences that will make you a better you.

People often ask me if I ever have bad days because my message is always positive and upbeat. I typically laugh in response, and then share how often I wake up grumpy in the morning, feel guilty about yelling at my kids, and how PMS makes me want to eat everything in sight and then whine about it. Of course, I have bad days. I also know that bad days are temporary and new hope comes in the morning. I know that I have the power within me to change my attitude and how I receive things. I know that whatever happens today just might be a part of my story tomorrow so I do my best to take a bird's eye view at the situation and ask myself if it will really matter next week, next month, or in ten years.

Will my struggle today matter when I am facing the end of my life? More times than not, the answer is *no*. As with all things, I have not mastered any of this 100 percent of the time. Some days I still want to be Mommy Crankypants and some days I don't have the energy to fix my attitude so I sit with it and eat popcorn. But most days, I am seeking the good, the lesson, the growth that comes with all of it. That's what makes me *lucky* or someone who gets to experience *cool sh*t*. It's an open heart, an open mind, and the spirit of adventure. We're only on this earth for a short time. I want to make the most of it.

Remove judgement

Having an open heart and mind also helps us to see other people differently and meet them where they're at. I consider myself to be pretty liberal, and no we are not going to talk politics here. I am liberal in the sense that I respect and empathize where people are at during any given stage of their lives, even when I may not agree with their choices. I understand that their past is different from mine, as is their future.

Whether I will be spending a season or a lifetime knowing this person, I don't know. What I do

57

know is that whatever experiences they have had in their life have led us to the point of doing life together today—in this moment. It is not my place to judge one way or another who they are as a person, how they live, their opinions or beliefs, how they worship, where they work, and so on.

My one and only responsibility when doing life with someone, even if I am only standing in line with them at the grocery store, is to smile and shine my light on their life. I don't know what they're going through or what they have been through so I hold no expectations. My heart is open to receiving each moment and each encounter as it comes, knowing that every encounter is a piece of the spider web of life.

Unless someone is causing intentional harm toward myself or someone else, I try hard to not form an opinion about them unless it's one of love and respect or admiration. My opinions of right and wrong

58

are based on what I deem okay or not okay for my personal life but I do not put those expectations on the lives of others.

Our lives are individual. The way we are made up, wired to think, groomed to believe, and how our experiences have led us to this place are all different. It is not my job to judge how you live your life and I wouldn't expect it to be your job to judge mine. I am empathetic to the struggles that you have been through, the victories you've triumphed, and the experiences you've had. My heart is open to understand how you may be able to bless my life or how I may bless yours.

Each moment is a gift and each conversation is a blessing. Every time we make a new friend or meet someone at a mom's group or group fitness class, we have the opportunity to connect. Connection is what holds us all together in the grand life plan.

The easiest way to drop judgement is to find common ground. You may differ with someone when it comes to how they discipline their children but you might know how hard it is to be a mom and that's something you can relate to. You might not agree with someone's choice to marry a different race or the same gender but you know what true love feels like and that is something you can understand. Maybe you don't agree with the weight loss shake or nail polish your friend is selling on Facebook but you know what it's like to need to bring in more money to your family and put food on the table so you can respect their hustle. Maybe you don't agree that your sister co-sleeps with her children but you know what it's like to have sleepless nights and be willing to do anything to get some rest so you can agree to disagree.

Whatever it is, we all connect in some way and I am almost certain that if you look at things through a different lens, you can find common ground and understanding, respect, and even admiration for the choices of another. We're all in this life together, giving it all we've got, working every day to try to be the best we can be at all the roles we have been blessed with. The last thing we need is judgement—not on us and not in our hearts.

Choose empathy

In my business, I deal with women from all around the United States and Canada. I have teammates from diverse cultures, ethnicities, and backgrounds. Early in my career as a coach, I had no idea how to lead anyone and very little understanding of how to communicate with others, especially those with different cultures and backgrounds. Needless to say, my first two years were a lot of trial and error, a lot of apologies, and a few tears as I tried to navigate my way in the world of business through the internet.

I am a big proponent for failing forward and learning from our mistakes. I took each time that a conversation or a business relationship didn't go as expected to learn how I could become better for the next opportunity. My best friend, Lauren, is one of the most empathetic and understanding people I know. She has been my right-hand man through all of this and every time I would have a falling out with someone, she always reminded me to try to understand where they're coming from or to put myself in their shoes.

I still am learning how to lead every day but in the four-plus years I have been in this career, I've learned one key truth: Everybody just wants to be heard, understood, and loved where they're at. So that's what I do. I make every effort to not judge, to never criticize, to choose my words wisely, and to always empathize. I may not understand every person's point of view but I keep an open mind and remind myself that I don't walk in their shoes so I can't expect them to walk in mine. We must meet each other where we're at with open arms and the desire to listen.

Open your mind to change

Remember when Facebook didn't exist? Remember when Myspace was the thing? Remember when AOL Instant Messenger and chat rooms were the places to be? Or better yet, remember when the internet wasn't a part of your everyday life? What if we were all closed off to these new and weird ideas in the 1990s and 2000s? Chances are you wouldn't be reading this book because I sell it on Amazon and promote it through social media. I have no idea what I would be doing with my life because my entire livelihood is built on the internet at this point. It's a good thing you or your parents were open-minded enough to try this whole internet craze. I remember when my aunt told me about Google for the first time. I laughed and said *what the heck is a google?!* I am certain that most of us never thought Google would become a verb that we use in everyday language or that we would be tied to our cell phones every day whether it be personal life or business. '90s kids like me couldn't wait to get that Zack Morris giant cell phone one day!

Life changes every day. Technologies change, the way we do business changes, relationships change. We no longer have to ask a friend if they know the new person we want to date. We just have to look him up on Facebook or Google him to make sure he doesn't have any lingering police reports. The way we do life changes all the time. I love when *Millennials*

64

get made fun of for being Millennials like it's a bad thing. Sure, there are some Millennials who do feel a sense of entitlement but that's not exclusive to any one generation. Yes, we love to talk via the internet and spend a lot of time in social media and yes, there actually is an app for everything. Well, almost everything.

There are also thousands, if not hundreds of thousands, of us who are hustlers and using the internet and the world of apps to better our lives and the lives of those around us. Being a Millennial is kind of awesome. We're the generation of technology and change and if technology is used correctly, for good, and with an open mind and heart, the best things can be born of it. Change can be a good thing.

I often get lightheartedly made fun of for posting so much of my life on social media. My parents and friends of my family will joke about how much Krystle puts on Facebook about herself and her journey. I laugh back and remind them that I run a business from the comfort of my Facebook, thank you very much. But more than running a business, I build relationships.

I started sharing my journey on Facebook because I needed a place to check in in the early days of my weight-loss journey. I didn't expect much to come of it but I just wanted a place that would make me feel accountable and I was okay if only my mom would see the post. It was public and it served me well so even though it didn't make a whole lot of sense, I ran with it. It worked for me and that's all I needed— something to work.

To my surprise, people I had never met before started following my Facebook posts and encouraging my journey. It wasn't long before I had built an audience and soon after, I started to make friends from all around the world. Our wedding is this year and my maid of honor and officiant are both friends I met through Facebook years ago.

I've also built what I consider to be a successful business through Facebook and social media. I have been able to be home with my children while using my platform to inspire women across the world and, in turn, build a career in the process. There is no telling what my life would look like if I was closed off to the idea of sharing my journey on Facebook but I am certainly happy that I was open to receiving change.

Chances are that most of you reading this have already adapted to the world of the internet and Facebook. My point in all of this is that we must go through life knowing that it's always changing. Sure, you can be the one person who never adapts to societal changes, but I personally don't find adapting and changing to be such a bad idea most of the time. Adjusting to the way society and the world change and having your heart open to the goodness that wants to flow into it is how we evolve and grow as individuals and with each other. I want to stay connected to how the lives of those around me can bless my life and vice versa.

Who knows where we will be in another ten years. We will probably be able to telepathically transmit thoughts across the country and have pizza dropping out of drones. Wherever we are, my heart remains open because there are lessons in every season, people I need to meet, and opportunities in every encounter. I will only experience them when I am open to them. I hope that the person on the other end of that meeting is open to me as well.

Protect your peace

All of this said, I do not live in a fantasy world. I understand that life is not made up of rainbows and lollipops all of the time and sometimes things go awry. I understand that not all relationships stand the test of time and sometimes all the empathy in the world can't fix some people's level of crazy or disrespect.

Everybody who comes into your world is not meant to stay in your world and just as I have been open to receiving love and new relationships, I have also been willing to shut them down when it's needed. There have been people who have come into my life, and while knowing them was good at the time, as the seasons changed, having them in my life began to transform into baggage.

I will say this time and time again—protecting your peace is an inside job. So, while I talk about opening your heart, I also want you to remember that ~~it's okay to close your heart as well when it's needed.~~

You don't have to be walked all over for the sake of being open-hearted and nonjudgmental. You're not a doormat. When you are pursuing a higher life, a better life, a life of goodness and all that the universe has for you, there will be people who want to crush your dreams. There will be people who will want to see you fail and will do anything in their power to bring you down. People will begin to cast their own doubts, insecurities, and negative feelings onto you and while I am all for being a good friend, I am not an advocate of sacrificing your wellbeing or your peace.

It is hard to do. It's hard to break ties with people especially if they're close to you or if you have a lot of energy invested in them already. More often than not, they won't make it easy either. Deciding to close your heart is often a harder job than deciding to

70

open it. You'll know in your heart of hearts when the time is right. It doesn't happen often and you may only ever have to do it once. I pray that you'll never have to do it at all. But I want you to know that there is no shame in making decisions that better protect your wellbeing.

When you can put down the baggage, it frees up your arms so that you can better embrace the people who deserve and appreciate your love. The same goes for opportunities and situations that may be hindering your wellbeing. Obviously, not everybody can up and quit the job that they hate but you can be continuously pursuing joy and the things that do fuel and empower you, the things that bring you to life. Do what you can, when you can, with the resources you have to protect your inner wellbeing and be damned proud of the fact that you love yourself enough to do so.

"We cannot live only for ourselves. A thousand fibers connect us with our fellow men; and among those fibers, as sympathetic threads, our actions run as causes, and they come back to us as effects."

— *Herman Melville*

U: Unleash the Strongholds

When she's young, she's told that she's a princess.

That she can do anything and she will achieve success.

She's told she deserves the world and all that it has to bestow.

That she will learn many lessons, and from them she must grow.

A little girl believes deep inside that she is beautiful.

She believes she can do it all because she is powerful.

She's taught that beauty runs deeper than her skin,

That beauty comes from deep down in her soul,

From the person who lies within.

As a little girl, she's full of ambition and self-respect.

Knowing that her mind and body she must protect.

As that little girl becomes a young adult,

She comes across negativity and hate,

And subtly changes as a result.

In the midst of the confusion, she loses sight of what she used to know so well.

She is engrossed in society's standards and the notion that sex sells.

The young woman changes who she is and becomes someone new.

Being the girl on TV is a challenge she now must pursue.

So she lets go of the things instilled so long ago,

to fit in with everyone else and expand her ego

Beauty becomes having nice hair and clear skin,

big breasts, a long neck and a flat chin.

Success becomes winning high school's "best dressed"

conforming to her peers and leaving out her own "zest".

She now becomes so wrapped up in material things,

that she is no longer aware of her natural blessings.

The wall that was built protecting her own,

has slowly been broken down stone by stone.

One day she grows up and remembers being a little girl,

back when she believed she was as precious as a pearl.

She finds herself in awe at how she lost sight,

and now her womanly rules, she must rewrite.

So, she tells herself again,

that she is beautiful, powerful, and amazing,

that this is a beautiful life she is living.

Of course, she has been through struggles,

So, it's not as simple as before,

Past, present, and future, she now juggles.

She searches for that princess crown she once wore.

Once she was told and believed, no questions asked.

Now she must convince herself that this is the present, not the past.

Remember how she wholeheartedly believed she deserved the whole world,

Remind herself that deep down in her soul she is still that little girl.

That she is absolutely gorgeous inside and out,

That she can do anything she wants no matter how much they doubt.

That she is stronger than she thinks she can be,

That she can cleanse herself of that societal debris.

She is strong.

She is powerful.

She is beautiful.

She is a woman.

By Krystle J Bailey

Remember when I told you about looking for that contentment all around the world only to find it in my heart? Prior to meeting Nick, I was looking for love anywhere I could find it. Those tough times I mentioned were grueling, and I will own up to my part in them and say that even when I met him, he could

76

never do enough for me. In my mind, he could never love me the way I wanted to be loved, the way I needed to be loved, the way I thought love looked.

In my eyes, he was great but he could be greater. I knew he loved me but I wanted more and I let him know all the time that he needed to do more to show me love. I always found fault in him and would tell him what he could be doing better for me. I'd ask for more gifts, more time, more words, more everything and nothing ever filled the need to capacity.

Until a moment of healing that took place while I was sitting with God, heart wide open, seeking understanding. In this moment, I realized that it wasn't how he was loving me that was not right or enough—it was me not being able to fully accept true love even when it was right in my face. I was incapable of accepting true, unconditional, never-wavering, all-your-might love because I did not think I was worthy.

Here's the thing though: I didn't even know that I didn't think I was worthy. I told myself I was worthy. I said it out loud. All the personal development books, seminars, YouTube videos, podcasts about affirmations and self-confidence couldn't do it for me. I still hadn't believed in the depths of my soul that I was worthy of that love. Understanding why and freeing myself of these strongholds happened in a moment. Well, it happened moment after moment but all encompassed in one afternoon of inward reflection.

My parents divorced when I was five. I saw my dad often over the years and when I was twenty-one, he passed away. The same summer that I met Nick, my dad passed away of a sudden heart attack at forty-three years old. My entire world shattered. In the beginning, I cried all the time. I cried big, hard, ugly tears for several weeks until I learned that I was pregnant with my daughter and I had to stand up and carry on for the sake of the health of my unborn baby.

Over the course of those years that followed, I had stopped crying. I did not allow myself to feel emotions about my dad. Until I felt a tugging at my heart that there was healing needed to be done, grieving that needed to happen. It was an undeniable tugging. It had been seven years since he passed and I really thought I was okay. I had learned to just move on. I did everything within my power to avoid feeling the emotions, and I put off even thinking about my dad for too long.

That was my defense mechanism. If I didn't think about him, I wouldn't have to feel the feelings. I had built walls around him that wouldn't even allow me to look him in the eyes in pictures. If I didn't spend time in silence, I didn't have to heal. Every time I thought about him, I pushed the feelings back into the darkness and went about what I was doing. With an ice-cold heart, I could tell someone that my dad had passed away years ago. I could talk about him in passing with friends or family without feeling a thing. I had completely blocked out any feelings that were there to be felt as if they did not need to exist anymore.

I carried on about my life for years never thinking too long about my father. Until I came to a place that the tugging was so strong I could not focus on anything else. I argued with God about not wanting to deal with it. I told God how I didn't have time to feel feelings. I didn't have time to cry or think or be sad. I knew grieving had to happen but I just did not want to. But I had to. And when I did, it wasn't just grieving for my dad that happened. It was healing on deep levels that flooded my spirit and showed me something I had been looking for for years in all the wrong places. Things began to make sense.

When the time came that I could not do anything other than face my feelings, I first sat down and prayed. I sat with God and I turned to the first page of one of those adult coloring books. My mom had given me one for Christmas that was filled with scripture. I pulled out my colored markers and sat in silence while I reflected and allowed myself to feel. I vowed to myself that if the tears came, I'd let them flow. I would feel whatever was there for me in that moment.

1 John 3:1 was the scripture. "See what kind of love the Father has given to us that we should be called children of God and so we are." I repeated it over and over. I memorized it. I colored it. I reflected on it. I wrote in the margins, "I am loved." I wrote, "I am worthy of love." I said the same things I have been telling myself for years but this time I began to feel it. I

began to really allow myself to feel the love of my Heavenly Father first.

When I was soaked in God's love, I dug up the strength to pull up photos of my earthly father. For the first time in seven years, I looked him in the eyes and I was angry. Anger was not at all what I had anticipated feeling. I was bitter and I didn't know why. My instinct was to put away the pictures and put my wall back up, but I forced myself to feel all the feelings in the way that I knew I needed to if I was going to heal and grow from there. I sifted through pictures of him and me when I was a baby, when I was a child, when I was a teenager, and into the years leading up to his death. I looked him in the eye in everyone and as I did, my heart began to change. I began to see my dad's love for me.

I am not sure exactly where or when it happened but what I realized in that moment was that somewhere along the course of my life, I had told myself that my dad didn't *really* love me. And that I wasn't worthy of real love. As I sorted through the pictures and prayed, reflected, meditated, I realized how wrong I was. I saw love in those pictures. I thought of memories with my dad that I had buried so deep and I began to understand that my dad loved me in the best way he knew how. All these years, I had been handcuffed in thoughts that simply weren't true. The reality was that I held the key to my handcuffs; I just had to find it.

I called my mom that day. I asked her the tough questions. We talked for an hour about my childhood. I asked her to be honest with me about the things she meant, said, and did. A very simple breakthrough happened that day that took me years to discover and it all began with me sitting in silence with no expectations other than to be still. In that conversation, my mom asked me how I felt about my dad when I thought about him. My response to her was that I had a hard time differentiating between how I felt about him and how I felt I should feel about him because of her feelings.

Because my mom was honest with me for so many years and didn't hide things from me, I had taken on so many of her feelings. My mom is the best mom I could ask for. She did her best as a single mom knowing what she knew. She never would do anything intending to harm me. It wasn't until I was twenty-nine years old that I realized and could identify that her honesty policy when it came to my dad was not constructive to my ten-year-old heart, my twelve-year-old mind, or my fifteen-year-old self confidence. Because I love my mom so deeply and because this is how kids function, I realized in that moment that the feelings I had built surrounding my dad were not 100 percent my own. My feelings were partly my mom's.

At the end of our conversation, my mom said one sentence that changed the course of the rest of my life in an instant. She said, "I have never doubted your dad's love for you. He loved you more than anything in this world in the best way that he knew how." When I hung up the phone, I sat in silence for a few moments soaking in that truth. I was loved. I am loved. I am worthy of love.

My world opened that day. I had subconsciously held on to a false truth that I was unloved and unlovable. I did want more from my dad than he had to offer. I wanted more time. I also took on many of my mom's feelings about my dad. A combination of experiences led me to a place where my mind believed I wasn't worthy of love. I blame no one. My parents did the best they knew how and nobody can fault them for that. While writing this book, a text that I sent to my mom stated:

"The conversation that we had about my dad allowed serious healing to take place. Thank you for that. I am writing and I don't know what will make it into the book but I just want you to know that I respect everything you have ever done to be the best mom to me. I did take on some of your feelings about him and I've freed myself from that, which has allowed me to truly embrace Nick in a way that I never have before. I don't want you to feel bad about it though. You have molded me in a way and my life has shaped me in a way that is allowing God to use me for greatness. My pain is my victory."

That day when Nick came home, for the first time in the seven years we had been together, he was not just the man I wanted to marry but he was everything and more for me. He was enough for me in every sense of the word because it wasn't he who had changing to do. It was me and it began in silence and intentional spiritual nourishment.

This is one of my stories. There are countless other moments of my life that I have experienced and that I am sure, are yet to be experienced as I continue to grow, in which I will need to release myself from false truths.

You may have heard the analogy about elephants. Some refer to it as baby elephant syndrome. When a baby elephant is born in an environment of captivity whether it be the circus or some other environment other than the wild, it is tied by its ankle to a post or a tree stump. Because of the nature of an elephant, it tries to roam but as a baby, it is not strong enough to break free. Realizing that its efforts are useless, the baby elephant eventually gives up and succumbs to life attached to the post. As the elephant grows in size and strength, the elephant could easily uproot the same post it has been tied to for years but the elephant doesn't know that. The elephant believes that it cannot break free. The elephant believes what it is taught as a child—that when the rope is tied, it is stuck. The powerful beast that the elephant is is limited by its mind based on limitations and truths created as a child.

In the same way, many of us hold on to limitations or truths that we created as children and have never let go of. Deep in our minds, we are tied by the ropes that can so easily be broken if we are just shown that we are strong, capable, and mighty. We choose to believe what is not true because it's what we grew up believing. Until someone takes the blinders off and shows you otherwise.

What truths are you holding on to? How did they get there? What is keeping you in chains? And in the words of Tony Robbins, "When did you decide to accept that limitation for your life?"

Whatever it is, it is time to bless it and release it. It's time to let it go. It's time to live free. I talked about meditation as a means of opening your heart. Meditation is also a great way to let go of the things that are handcuffing you. Recently, I had a powerful experience and the honor of meditating with a group of open-minded individuals in a tiki hut in Punta Cana, Dominican Republic. Rain was pouring down around the tiki while fifteen of us sat in silence after some guidance in meditation by a former Green Beret in the United States Army.

Adam has since retired from Special Forces and now works with warriors through the Save a Warrior project. After Adam came home from service, he found himself with PTSD and depression and thoughts of suicide. Learning the power of meditation saved

89

Adam's life and now he works to save the lives of others by teaching this practice. Every day, the members of this organization are helping warriors, as well as those in any traumatic career such as fire fighters, police, and other first responders, through the power of meditation so that they can heal and begin to take back their life.

Through this warrior meditation, the goal was to essentially remove yourself from your cognitive state and immerse yourself into full meditation, allowing thoughts to come and go like flowing water and just go freely wherever your mind would take you. After we finished a twenty-minute meditation, the floor was open to discussion. Women shared how they found themselves at the top of a mountain releasing words of self-doubt, negativity, anger, and bitterness off the edge. Adam shared different techniques of releasing these thoughts such as visualizing the limiting thoughts as leaves flowing down a stream that get stuck on a rock, only to be washed away a second or so later or putting your thoughts into bottles and releasing them into the ocean.

Whatever visual is used is personal to each individual but the healing comes by releasing it all. The poison that we hold on to that holds us back from living a true life of wellness. You don't have to be a first responder or to have served in the military to have wounds and struggles that you need to overcome. We all have things that we hold on to that limit us, that hurt us, that we need to heal from. Acknowledging that healing is necessary is the first step in living free of the chains. You deserve freedom, sister. Break the chains.

Motivational speeches work, meditation works, and so does prayer. Prayer always works. I attended a women's conference that rocked my world in the way of releasing strongholds. The speaker led us through an activity as she spoke about the nametags that we wore underneath our clothes. She shared how she had been bullied in school and even though she had grown to be a well-loved, accepted, and admired pastor's wife and motivational speaker, that for years she still carried the name *Rejected* on an imaginary nametag under the nametag that read, *Allison.* She held on to a false truth that was created as a child. As she walked us through this conversation, she challenged us to write down the names that we had been holding on to that didn't belong to us. *Fat, Ugly, Rejected, Unworthy, Useless, Nothing, Unloved* were some of the names women wrote. We were then reminded that when God calls us, he doesn't call us by those names. He calls us by our name. He doesn't whisper, *"Hey, Fat! Come to me."* He whispers your name. He didn't ask *Whore* to write this book. He asked Krystle to write the book. That day, I laid down my false names. I laid down *Whore,*

Fat, and Unloved. I laid them down at the altar and when I laid them down, I picked up three truths. I picked up, *Beautiful, Saved, and Redeemed.* I left that day renewed. I freed myself of false truths, false names, things that I had held on to since I was a child and teenager that did not define me. Not only did they not define me now but they never did.

I am Krystle. I am a child of the one true King. You are a child of the one true King and you are not any of the negative name badges you might still be wearing. It is okay to lay them down. This is your invitation to lay them at the altar, to let them go like leaves flowing down a stream, or words falling off a mountain top. This is your invitation to let go of who you've been telling yourself you are and embrace your most authentic, beautiful, worthy, loved self. That is the version of yourself the world needs.

R: Realize Your Truths

Peel back the layers
Go a little deeper
Dig a little further
The vision's becoming clearer
Break free from the chains
Dive deeper still
Stay focused on the mission
Move delicately through the mill
Look, there ahead
It's coming into view
Do you see her yet?
She's the best version of you.
By Krystle J Bailey

For entirely too long, I lived in a world where I thought I had to be something I was not. I lived next door to the *Joneses of Weight Loss.* Then I moved in next door to the *Joneses of Business.* Let me tell you this—trying to keep up with either of them was utterly exhausting but it taught me a thing or two about who I really am. Often times we need to learn who we are not in order to really understand who we are.

My time spent trying to keep up with the Joneses of Weight Loss will be covered more in the chapter on struggles but let me give you a little insight into that part of my story. In 2010, after giving birth to my beautiful baby girl, Elliana, I set out to lose weight. I wanted to feel better and live better for my daughter. At almost 300 pounds when I gave birth to her, I knew there had to be change on the horizon. She was my life and it was my responsibility to be the best I could.

I started my weight loss journey with a company I was familiar with. It taught me how to eat less of the things I loved and still be able to go out to eat, go to parties, and enjoy things like pizza on occasion. I wanted to lose fifty pounds. If I could get to around 200 pounds, I thought, then I would be happy, life would be good, and I'd be back to about where I was in high school. In the process of losing that fifty pounds, I found myself in a race that I don't remember signing up for.

I was surrounded by people on the internet who were also on their own weight loss journeys, and I found myself trying to keep up with them. I started running because they were running. I started changing my goals because they were changing their goals. I started doing things they were doing because it seemed like the right thing to do. The program I was using at the time, told me that my weight loss goal should be under 150 pounds, which meant losing 100 pounds, so I did it. I was on a mission and the mission was to be healthy for my daughter so if they said that was healthy then I pushed. And I pushed, and I pushed, and I pushed. Until I broke.

Along the way I had lost sight of what I was really doing this for and why. I reached my goal of weighing 150 pounds and continued to push the limits wondering what it would feel like to lose just five more pounds, just two more pounds, and so on. I ran 5Ks and 10Ks and obstacle races, I wore single-digit jeans, I wore a size two, I hit every goal there was to hit until I was utterly exhausted and I found myself in a place that I never in a million years thought I would be. I was skinny. I was skinny and I was depressed. I was sad and cranky and at war in my mind. We will pick this story back up in the next two chapters.

It was in the midst of all of this that I also got into business in the area of health and fitness. Again, starting with good intentions, I quickly found myself running a new race. This time I was chasing recognition and awards, but not really understanding why or with what intention other than I just desired to be good at things. Prior to the weight loss, I had never achieved anything significant in my life.

My "truth" (reference conversation about strongholds) was that I was placed on this earth to hold a warm place. When I lost over one hundred pounds, I had experienced the sweet aroma of achievement. This was it. This was my season, my moment, the underdog victory. I was high on achievement and I loved the cheers of victory.

Have you ever walked into a restaurant that gave off the sweetest aroma, only to try the food and be sadly disappointed in the taste? That's what all of this became to me when I came down from the high. For about four years of my life, I was running the race. I was trying to keep up. I was chasing the sweet sweet smell that was emanating from the ideal of achievement whether it was in the area of weight loss, fitness, or business and recognition. I had tasted a lick of what I thought was success and I wanted more.

After four years of running, I slowed down to have my son, my second born. It was in that slow season that I realized how tired I was. I realized how much I had been chasing after something that I didn't even really know I wanted. Do I want success? Absolutely! Don't we all? But my perception of success and what I wanted was all wrong. It didn't align with my priorities and it certainly didn't keep my priorities well nourished.

It was when I slowed down that I began to realize my truths. I took time off from everything except my family when I had my son. When it was time to *get back in the race*, I decided that I was done. I didn't want to chase things anymore. I didn't want to force anything that didn't belong in my life anymore. I wanted to learn who I was meant to be in this season of my life. I knew that I simply didn't have the energy to keep up with anyone so I had to figure out what success, life well lived, and a fulfilled purpose looked like for Krystle and nobody else.

This truth-seeking journey would prove to be unchartered territory. Being yourself in a world where we are constantly being bombarded with the idea that we should be something else is the biggest challenge known to modern day women. Seeking my truth meant that I had to be okay with not getting back to a certain size or weight because being that size required me to be in extreme diet mode. It meant that if it wasn't meant for me, I might not achieve [Insert business milestone here]. It also meant that I would have to learn to be okay with not achieving a new milestone *all* of the time. It meant that I would have to learn to be

100

okay with just being and that just *being* could be as enjoyable as, if not more enjoyable than, achieving.

I learned how to be a human *being* and not a human *becoming*. I learned that I really love being a mom and a wife more than anything else in this world, that I could be good at things that had nothing to do with my body or my weight, that in the midst of chasing achievement I had actually learned so many other great traits but I just wasn't focusing on them so they lay dormant.

Seeking your truth is a workout for the mind and soul. It comes on an internal level and cannot be influenced by anybody or anything else. I had to get real with myself and I continue to have to check my intentions, as we are always works in progress on any path of life. I spoke about social media as a blessing if you allow it to be. It can also be a curse if you allow it to be.

101

In a world where everyone is an entrepreneur and a fitness model and a business owner and an author and the best mom, the best wife, the best every damn thing, it's easy to lose yourself in the mix. Realizing your truth is about identifying who you are in the midst of it all and staying true to that. It's about identifying who you are as a woman, who you are as a mom, a wife, in whatever career that you choose, and so on. It's about identifying it, clearly defining it, and embracing it. It's okay to just be you.

I don't know about you but I tend to find that when I decide to change my life in a new way, I am almost instantaneously faced with some sort of challenge in that area. It's almost as if I claim something in the name of the Lord for my life and then He says, *Hey, let's test that theory, little lady.*

So I made this decision to begin living for me and stop running these proverbial races. Insert first challenge in truth seeking. Shortly after I had my son, I was added to a bunch of Facebook groups about breastfeeding or what were known as "crunchy mom groups" meaning moms who love all things organic and pure.

Before I get into this, hear me out—these moms are incredible moms! They care so much for their children, what they eat, how they make their baby food, what kinds of swaddles they use, how they nurse their babies, what formulas they would never use, when to start solid foods, how they travel, what car seats they use, and so on. They are loving, caring, compassionate moms and they are rock stars and I am *so* not one of them. I am a hot mess mom making it work on a whim. I'm also not afraid to admit it.

As soon as I began to question things about myself as a mom though, I had to leave those groups. Not because I didn't think those women were incredible because no matter how you cut it, being a mom is a hard job and they're rock stars for putting so much extra TLC into it, but more often than not, I found myself questioning if I was doing a good enough job as a mom, if I should change everything I know to do it a different way, if maybe I raised my daughter *wrong* by not doing it their way. Once the doubt crept in and the comparison planted its seed, I had to go.

Rather than staying and feeling negative emotions about myself as a mom, as if parenting isn't hard enough, I decided that I would respect those moms from a distance and realize and embrace that I'm a hot mess mom and that's alright! I love my kids unconditionally and that is enough. The moment I clicked "Leave Group", I proclaimed one of my truths out loud. I said, "I am a great mother."

I could give example after example about this but I think by now you get the idea and you have probably pieced together that comparison has been a weakness of mine for a long time. I tend to get easily caught up in what the next person in my field is doing. So, in order to truly live out my own truth, I safeguard myself from situations that might allow me to fall into the comparison trap or negative feelings about myself. I am a big girl and I can make big girl decisions so I make it a priority that those decisions are based on what's best for me.

As selfish as that might sound, I know that when I am making those decisions for myself first, I am a better wife, mom, friend, mentor, writer and the list goes on. I can only be all of those things to the best of my ability when I am making it a priority to live boldly in my truth.

In the writing of this book, I've gone on an *input fast*, if you will. In an effort to protect my peace and continue to pursue my own truth through the birthing of this book, I thought it would be best if all of my writing came from what I already know, feel, believe, and have experienced. So while I am a big fan of personal growth books, audio, and seminars, as I got to the end of my writing, I turned it all off. I know that God has called me to this place for my purpose here on this earth. I know that He has already equipped me with all that I need to complete my mission. I know that my heart and mind are prepared to bring this to life.

There are incredible speakers and writers out there and when I am done writing, I will listen to them, as we are always works in progress. Right now, my growth is introspective and often, the input noise is so loud that we cannot hear the still small voice right there within us that is waiting to be heard.

The one book I did read as I wrapped up writing was a book called *Writing with Quiet Hands* by

Paula Munier. This solidified what I already knew in my heart—that my voice was meant to be heard and once I hone in on it, it can change the world, that using what I've learned from other writers and speakers is the beauty of art and creation, that my voice was unique for the readers I will connect with. It isn't about writing the perfect words, it's about allowing you to feel my heart.

Maybe you can relate to the fitness or the business race, motherhood and parenting, maybe you need to tune out the noise so you can listen to your heart, or a different personal challenge altogether but whatever it is, I want to encourage you to pursue what feels the most natural and rewarding for you. When you're alone at night in your bed, what makes you feel satisfied? If social media disappeared tomorrow and there were no more likes or comments to validate your thoughts, who would you be without it? If you don't

107

know, I want you to know that that's okay! Take this opportunity to think about it, write, pray, and reflect on it. Seek the things that make you feel at peace. Uncover it and then protect it with all of your might.

Your truth is special and unique to you. Nurture it and take care of it. It's what makes you who you are without all of the layers. All you need in life is already within you. Your peace, your happiness, your contentment are all within yourself. You don't need validation from anyone. As long as what you're doing at any given moment aligns with your true north, you're in the right place. You'll know it when you experience it. Just continue to pursue it. I truly believe that we make the world a little bit brighter when we all live boldly in the life that was given to us.

My dad wanted nothing but the best for me. He drilled into my head at an early age that I would go to college, I would do better than he did, I would work

108

hard, I would get an excellent job and I would provide for myself before I depended on any man. As I grew, I embodied that. That thought process evolved to include that I would never be a stay at home mom, I would always have my own money, I would never *sell my soul* to a man because I am an independent woman.

Note, you cannot decide what you'll do as an adult until you're actually an adult. You can't truly say what kind of parent you'll be until you're actually a parent. For a long time, I carried these grand plans with me until I became a mom and until my husband gave me the opportunity to stay at home with my children. I do work from home to bring an income to the household but my husband is my provider and protector.

It took me quite some time and a lot of prayer to break free of my dad's repeated lessons of what he expected for my life but in seeking my truth, I have found that not only am I okay with Nick protecting and providing for me but I actually enjoy *just* being a mom and wife. If all else faded away and I wasn't an author, a mentor, a coach, a social media persona, I would be content and at peace being a mom and wife.

That said, I believe that God gave me a voice for a reason and my responsibility is to use it for good. I am continuing to pursue what else my truth has in store for me, and a big piece of that is birthing this book. It's going all the way back to the thing that brought me joy when I was a young child and getting excited about it again. It's about touching the heart of my mother with my writing and then well beyond. When I began writing, my heart was going at ten thousand miles a minute as endorphins filled my brain. When I write a chapter that I love, my hands tremble and my heart races, I write with a smile on my face and my shoulders pulled back.

Sometimes, I get up and take a lap around the house just to shake the *giddy* feeling out because I am so excited to be in my zone and writing my truth. I am happy here. I'm happy with a pen in my hand, I am overjoyed when the pieces of a chapter fall into place, I snuggle up to my books about writing such as the one I mentioned by Paula Munier. When someone asks me about my writing, my face lights up as I tell them about how things are always changing, how exciting it is when I connect with my muse, the future I envision for my writing and upcoming books. This is how I know I am living in my truth. This is how I know that right here is where I need to be.

When things got real in my writing, I had to take a step back from another entrepreneurial business I manage so I could give my focus to making this book the best that it could be. A couple of people within that business had a tough time understanding my decision to do this. Opinions were expressed, negative conversations, and hurtful accusations were made about me and my decision to put my other business on the back burner for a little while.

In other circumstances, accusations and opinions like this would have made me question my decisions, but this particular instance was not one of them. Rather than doubting myself about all the things that were said about me, I made the conscious decision to stay in my lane and stay focused on what God needed me to be doing. These conversations and opinions were merely a distraction from me doing what is meant for me in this season, which is to write.

When you're living boldly in your truth, you know it and nobody can take it away from you. When you're living boldly in your truth, the opinions of others about what you are doing become nothing but

112

noise in the background. It's just you and your truth. Just the two of you.

Getting to this place typically doesn't prove to be an easy road. It usually involves speed bumps, failure, trying new things, hiccups along the way, self-doubt, time, energy, and a whole lot of effort. I have spent years trying to figure out what it could feel like to be one of those people who felt it in their heart of hearts when they said, *I love what I do.* Often, we will have to pass over steppingstones, spending time in different seasons so that we can be primed and prepared for when we arrive in our truth.

My advice to you, if you don't yet know what your truth looks like, is to be patient. Be patient and show yourself grace in each season of life. Pray every day and ask God to reveal to you the plans that He has for your life. Be open to the idea of steppingstones and know that it's okay for you to take a while getting to where you're going. Your story is in the journey. Most of all, learn to embrace who you are becoming in the process. The journey of life doesn't end until it's over so just begin to let your hair down and flow in and out of the seasons of life as they're handed to you. Love who you are today and be open to loving who you'll be tomorrow. You don't have to be perfect at any of this so learn from your mistakes and your failures and use them as fuel for the future successes. And even when you arrive in your *truth*, you still won't be perfect. Perfection is perception and who you are is a blessing.

Your truth might take some time to find but when you grab ahold of it, it's like a pair of jeans that you don't have to jump, wiggle, and shimmy into. It's the way a child playing with the geometric peg board finally finds the square hole for his square peg and it slips through with ease, as he spills over with joy. It's like the way your hand effortlessly fits with the one of the person you will one day marry. You know your truth when you feel it because things begin to make more sense in a new way than anything else has before. Realize that it doesn't typically come in a moment but in a series of moments, experiences, failures, mistakes, learned lessons, through meditation, prayer, and/or fasting. The way the world is set up, we're always being told to be something other than we are so realizing your truth is going to take some work on your part but it's worth the effort in more ways than I can put into words.

Here are some of my fun, more lighthearted, real, raw, keep it 100 percent truths:

It is my honor to serve my husband, but sometimes he drives me bananas. It is my pride to be a mom, and sometimes I lose my temper. I love Jesus, but sometimes I miss church. I love nutrition, but I love cocktails with friends. When I need to take the edge off, sometimes I meditate but most of the time, I pour a glass of wine. I'm an extrovert by nature, turned introvert as I age. I believe in the power of words, but I curse often. I am a working, hustling, loving, compassionate woman who sometimes has it all together and often is a hot mess. I change my hairstyle with the change of the wind. I can't just look at a thing as a thing, everything has a deeper meaning. Above all else, I really, truly like myself. I look in the mirror and I like what I see staring back at me not because of my physical appearance but because I know and connect with my most authentic self with eyes of grace, love, and forgiveness. I wouldn't change who I am for anything in this world. This is how God made me and I am embracing it, unapologetically, for the first time in my life.

This is my truth. What's yours? When you realize it, put your blinders on, stay in your lane, and embrace life in your truth for all that it has to offer you.

I: Invite God In

Embrace yourself
For exactly who you are
Embrace where you've been
You have come so far
Your past doesn't define you
Your experience refines you
You are a diamond in the rough
And who you are today is enough.
Perfection is perception
What's perfect is your reflection.

Look at yourself today
In all of your beauty and grace
Your "flaws" make you unique
Perfectly imperfect, so to speak.
You are as you as you can be
Being so perfectly you is beautiful to me
So stop discounting your reflection
Hidden behind fears and rejection

118

Today, step out on faith
Knowing that you are washed in His grace.
By Krystle J Bailey

This isn't about religion or which church you should go to, how you should pray, or what you should believe. This is about a relationship with your creator. This is about my relationship with God and how it has transformed my life. I will be honest. Including my faith wasn't always a part of my message and I worried about including a whole chapter on faith but I will tell you this as simply as it gets: Without God, without faith, without my relationship with the Lord, there is none of this. There is no Krystle J Bailey, Author. All of this is for Him. To not include my faith in anything that I do at this point, would be robbing the world of the core of what I bring to the table and how I got to this place. I am not here to tell you how to believe or what's right from wrong and I understand and respect

119

how different belief systems can be. I want you to lose the notion of "religion" for this section of the book and read open mindedly. Just like every other topic in this book and in life, the way we worship might not be the exact same and that is just fine.

I'm not a pastor, a preacher, a prophet or a religious professional in any capacity. I am just a God girl who loves Jesus and loves what happens when you starve your doubt and nourish your faith.

The other three priorities I mentioned (mind, body, and relationships) are a little more objective than this one. Feeding and nourishing your spirit is something that can only be done through faith and on an internal level. We can read books that nourish our minds, eat foods that nourish our bodies, and have conversations that nourish our relationships and we will get into all of those things.

Nourishing our spirit is something that cannot be objectified as easily and takes true connection with oneself—something even harder to achieve. In order to truly be connected to the core of who we are, that requires stillness and silence. I don't know about you but as a woman and as a mother, being still and silent, while something we crave, is one our biggest challenges. Even when we have those rare moments where our kids are still sleeping and the house is quiet, we typically tend to fill the silence with noise whether we are making a mental to do list, thinking about a conversation we had in the past, worried about how we look, or thinking about how messy the house is, we are always filling our minds with noise. Being still and being silent is an art and the ability to create it comes from being okay with what you will experience there.

I have two kids and they love puzzles. They get puzzles every birthday and every Christmas and no matter how hard we try, the puzzles never make it long in our house. There are always pieces that go missing. My-two-year-old son will insist that we leave a puzzle put together on the floor and never put the pieces back in the box so without fail, the pieces go missing one by one. I'll find them in the bathroom, under the rug, tucked inside a book, or soaked in spilled juice. When I can't take the mess anymore, I begin to throw the pieces away. Half of them are ruined or missing and the rest are still half pieced together on the floor. The puzzle is rendered useless when I go on my cleaning spree and ends up tossed in the trash 95 percent of the time until the next puzzle makes its way through our door.

God doesn't throw our pieces away. I used to fear being quiet with myself and with God because I felt so broken. How could I bring myself to the God of the universe so broken and as such a hot mess? What

122

I've learned through faith is that you don't need to have your pieces together. You can bring your juice-soaked, dusty, broken puzzle pieces in a crinkled-up paper bag with you when you sit with God, and in your silence, in your brokenness, is where He will meet you and where healing will begin. That is where He begins to make a masterpiece of your broken pieces.

Trust me, I know how scary it is to think about silence. The writing of this book was prolonged exponentially because of my fear of being still, silent, and by myself long enough to actually write. I knew I wanted to ask God what He needed me to write about but there were places of self-reflection I did not want to visit. I was used to covering my wounds with noise, busyness, responsibility, vices, and more. Actually sitting with them is a foreign concept in twenty-first-century womanhood but it is possible and I am here to encourage you to experience it.

I: Invite God In

This is your invitation to be still. This is your reminder that God can make a masterpiece of our messiness if we allow it and it begins with bringing all of our broken pieces and resting in what He can do. Nothing goes to waste. Invite Him in to have a relationship with you. He will love you where you're at. When you do this, you might find that you experience healing and rest in a way that you were not expecting. My most recent experience with this has broken down walls and allowed me to heal and finally break barriers that were hindering me from writing openly and loving freely.

That story about my dad and the healing I needed to experience came when I silenced my heart and mind enough to listen and connect. I don't know what it is that you have going on your heart but I know that silence, stillness, and moments of just being are an integral part of living a life of wellness.

We are all human and we carry brokenness with us as the years pass. We don't have to carry those burdens forever though. We can leave them at the foot of the cross. We can bless them into the universe and free ourselves of the weight on our shoulders. We can take care of our spirit and when we do, that frees us to take care of other areas of our life.

The power of a morning routine is so critical to my spiritual wellbeing and relationship with God. Waking up before the sun and the kids, before I am needed, before the noise of the world sets the tone for my entire day. It is my time to bring my broken pieces and just be. It's my time to not need to be perfect, to think freely, pray wildly, meditate, cry, write, read, or whatever satisfies my soul on any given day.

One thing I don't do is open my email, my Facebook, my messages, or anything that would require me to be needed in those moments. My

125

morning is my time to just be Krystle without borders, without apologies, without expectations. That time sets the tone for my entire day and allows me to confidently nourish my other three pillars of wellbeing.

During that time, I read devotionals on my YouVersion Bible app. I pray over what God needs me to hear and understand that day, open a devotional that speaks to my heart, and read the corresponding scripture. I read a personal growth book that has nothing to do with business but everything to do with my life. Something to set the tone for the person I desire to be for the day. I have a list of prayer topics. Some mornings I pray all of them, some mornings I pray more adamantly about just a few. My prayers include:

I ask God to help me to honor Him in all that I am and all that I do.

I pray for my marriage, my husband, our love, our commitment and ask for His guidance in being an obedient and loving wife.

I pray for my children, their wellbeing, their health, and my role as their mother. I ask for calmness of my spirit and my tongue, patience and understanding of their perspective on life, and the forgiveness ahead of time of where I know I will fall short.

I pray for the people I will come in contact with today, that our conversations and crossing of paths will be meaningful and important.

I ask God to help me to be intentional with my time, to grow a business that honors Him, to help me to speak life into others, and to allow my life to sing His praise.

I pray that we will be guarded with a shield of protection, love, and grace as we head out into the world today.

Spending this time in the morning provides a margin between sleeping and waking that makes the day go a little smoother. It flows together eloquently and prepares me to write my best story each day. It's fueled by coffee, Jesus, sweatpants, and the sunrise and it sets the tone for everything I aspire to be and everything I hope to do that day.

Of course, there are those random off days when I oversleep, the kids wake me up, and I am running late and those days start with, "Lord, just help me to be my best today! With you, I got this!!" Hey, I never claimed to be perfect.

I know what you're thinking. I thought it too. You're telling yourself the story of why you can't wake up earlier than you already do, how hard it is to get out of bed, how warm and comfy your bed is, and how sleep is just so glorious. Oh, trust me, I know. I will tell you this—getting out of bed and to the coffee pot is the hardest part!

If you want to start a morning routine, I would highly encourage you to read the book, *Miracle Morning* by Hal Elrod. He offers practical tips on creating a morning of abundance that will rock your world.

At this point, you know how comparison has robbed me of so much. This is no exception! My spirituality today looks different than it did a year ago and I anticipate that as I grow, it will continue to look different and continue to grow and evolve along with me. Too many times, I have found myself comparing my worship hands to the hands of the pastor's wife or feeling like I wasn't *doing it right* because I missed church for a month at a time. I've questioned if I was a good enough Christian if I did not give something up for Lent or physically pray on my knees or take my kids to Bible study or go to small groups. The list goes on.

People live out their faith in so many different ways that it is nearly impossible to do it all. I had to learn that it doesn't lessen my relationship with God if I am not teaching Sunday school. I am not less forgiven if I don't go to every season of the small groups hosted at church. I am not less redeemed if I take a season away from church to find one that serves me better. But for years I believed those things. For years, I believed I was less than the person who did it differently than I did. I didn't believe I was a good enough Christian any more than I believed I was good enough in other areas of my life.

My insecurity in who I was didn't discriminate against any one area of my life. So when it came to my spirituality, I would shy away from a true and real relationship with the God who loved me because I was too busy spending energy on what I wasn't doing *right* and feeling bad about it. Here's what I know: The way we connect with God is unique, the way we nourish our spiritual wellbeing is special to us, the way we worship is between God and ourselves.

Being a Christian is a religious title. At this point in my life, I don't really care if I raise one hand or two in worship or if I don't go to church at all if my spirit is well taken care of and I feel personally connected with Christ. That's what being a Christian means to me and it is okay that it might mean something else entirely to you. That's the beautiful thing about this life—we are all created as unique as the snowflakes that fall from the sky.

I asked a few women I am close with what nourishing their spirit meant to them personally. Their responses included:

"Nourishing my spirit is reading the Bible or a devotional, spending time in my prayer journal, talking to God about everything in my life. It's when I do all of these things that I feel spiritually nourished."

"As my life changes, this means different things to me. Nowadays, it's just being with my baby. The absolute best is sitting in a rocking chair in silence preferably by the lake. Just BE-ing. Essentially removing any pressure from my mind or heart. That's when I feel spiritually well."

"To me, nourishing my spirit means that I am spending time with my Heavenly Father. Anything from listening to worship music, reading my Bible, praying, and sometimes just being in silence and embracing myself while in His presence."

"Quiet time. Truly just sitting and doing something to fill my heart."

"To me, nourishing your spirit means doing things that make your soul feel good. I think it's different for different people but in general, for me, it's spending time with God, reflecting, giving thanks, doing good in the world, and loving on others."

S: Struggles Create Your

Story

Who I am is not defined by my flesh.

I see it in the mirror but what about the rest?

My eyes, they connect deeply.

My lips, they kiss sweetly.

My arms, they hug my family.

My hands, they write freely.

My shoulders, they comfort completely.

My stomach? It carried life within me!

My skin, it caresses gently.

My heart loves intensely.

My legs. This SOUL they carry.

My knees, on them I pray intently.

My feet carry me as I live fully.

I am not defined by my flesh, it's just what you see.

This body is a home for the life that lives within me.
By Krystle J Bailey

When I weighed 300 pounds I struggled. When I weighed 145 pounds I struggled. Struggle is not one size fits all. It doesn't discriminate. Struggle is a part of life. It's how we learn, how we grow, how we become who we were put on this earth to be. Tell me an inspiring story of someone who hasn't faced struggle at some point in their life. As a matter of fact, let me know if you know anyone who hasn't faced struggle in their life! You'd be hard pressed to find someone because struggle is a part of each and every one of our lives.

But struggle is what you make it. When we are in the trenches amidst the turmoil, we want to know *why me?* But what happens when you come out on the other side of the struggle is so beautiful. You're stronger. You're braver. You're wiser. You are an overcomer and while I realize that all of our struggles look different, I believe that your story and mine have crossed paths for a reason. I don't know what it is that you're going through right now but I know that if you wade through the storm and pray your way through it, you'll come out on the other side able to help someone else in another season of your life.

Your struggle is your story. Every good story has a plot, suspense, a climax, a hero. You can become your own hero by using your story for good. It might not be on a grand scale. It might be helping your next-door neighbor or relating to and understanding a friend in an intimate way. It might be mentoring a child or a colleague through something that you have overcome. Or maybe you're still in the trenches and you haven't quite overcome but you can band arms with someone else going through it so that they don't feel alone.

136

Whatever it is, I can assure you that there is a way to use your struggle for good and I can promise you that if you open your heart, you will find that you are not alone either.

While I have experienced many struggles throughout my life, my biggest has always been my weight. I told you a little bit about my weight loss story in *R: Realizing Your Truths* but I want you to really understand this because it has great significance in how we got here today.

I was always asked when I would write a book. I was losing my weight and sharing my journey and people asked me every day when I would write a book. In my heart of hearts, I knew that my story wasn't done unfolding but I didn't know what was over the horizon. I just knew that whenever I did write a book, it wouldn't be about weight loss alone so I had to wait it out and see where life took me.

137

From the time I was five, I can remember being overweight. I remember that feeling when I realized I wasn't like everyone else. I was different. My belly was bigger, I ate more than they ate, and I couldn't run as fast as they could. I was just a little different but I knew it. Later, the weight piled on and food became my comfort. It was my healer before I knew Jesus. It was my love before I knew true love. It was food and it was my jam. So , despite being relatively active as a kid, I was also significantly bigger than most of the kids around me.

Being overweight as a child and young adult packed so many layers of insecurities into my world. I would make negative comments about other people so they couldn't make them about me first. I remember to this day a moment in sixth grade when the one other girl who was heavier than the other kids admitted her weight in front of a group of friends. She and I were the same weight but I joined in the others' shocked response, as if I couldn't relate to her.

My insecurities ranged everywhere from talking about others to being sexually promiscuous with anybody who would show me attention at about age fifteen. I would take any attention I could get and was quick to give up my body for the sake of *love*. Remember what I laid down at the altar? *Whore* was the nametag I had given myself and it began in my teenage years when I was desperate to be more than just a *big girl*.

My senior year of high school, I lost about fifty pounds. I was going to school and working at Friendly's. I was dating a guy I worked with who was not good for me emotionally. I was losing weight for him, for attention, for love, for all the wrong reasons. He moved away my freshman year of college. I was young, dumb, and heartbroken and used to cry for him to come back.

He would bribe me and tell me that if I just hit that next weight loss goal, he would move back. If I just lost more weight, he would move back. I am fairly certain he thought it was a good motivating factor and I am still friendly with him to this day. I don't think he really knew how deeply he was hurting me and that he wasn't motivating me at all, rather making me feel like my worth depended on my weight. Whether I would lose the weight and he would move back, I'd never find out because I proceeded to gain all of my weight back plus some over the course of the next couple of years. That's typically the case when you do big things for all the wrong reasons—they don't last.

In my senior year of college, which I say very loosely because it took me six years to graduate, my life changed for all the right reasons. I met Nick and we were soon pregnant with our daughter. When I gave birth to her in 2010, I was almost 300 pounds but more than just being overweight, I was unhealthy. I had an unhealthy relationship with food and body image and I knew that wasn't what I wanted as a mom. I wanted to do better by my baby girl and that was a reason worth fighting for. She became my *why* and eventually I became my *why*.

I remember the day as clearly as if it were yesterday when the switch flipped. My daughter was two months old. I had just spent the day playing with her and staring into her big, beautiful brown eyes, thinking about how crazy it was that I was a mommy. We were driving home from Nick's parents' house and my heart was heavy. I turned to him and I said, "I've gotta change. I can't live like this for her. I have to lose weight and I have to do it now."

And so began my weight loss journey. I proceeded to lose 100 pounds and found myself in the race that I mentioned—the one I didn't realize I was running to keep up with the *Joneses of Weight Loss* and what I understood to be *healthy*.

Healthy competition can be a good thing, sure but I wasn't in a healthy competition. I was in an unhealthy race to the finish that didn't exist with people who may or may not have been in competition with me. I don't know because the judge lived between my own two ears. The start, the race, the finish line all lived within me. I was pushing against the girl who lost five pounds in my meeting that week. I was trying to keep pace with the woman who started after me but lost more than I had. I was busting my back to run a little farther so I could post on social media that I did more that day. I was in a race of doing more and being more. Not just more than the girl next to me but more than the person I was yesterday.

Every day I felt this burning desire to prove something to someone. It began as a journey to prove something to myself—that I could do this once and for all and that I could live better for my daughter. I can't tell you the exact moment that it became all of these other things but I was knee-deep in weight loss quicksand before I realized it.

My journey didn't start out this way. The majority of the first year was all good things. I was positive and excited about the changes I was making. I loved feeling alive and lighter in so many ways. I loved what I was doing for myself and for my family. It wasn't until a year or so into it that things began to really take a turn for the worse.

I used to cry when the scale didn't change from one morning to the next. I would skip on get-togethers

143

with friends if it meant hindering my weigh-in. I'd sweat as much as possible the day before I knew I had to get on the scale, not leaving the gym until at least 1,000 calories were burned. The night before my weekly weigh-ins, I would dehydrate myself so the scale would be a half of a pound lighter in the morning. I would face the scale with as few clothes on that I could publicly get away with, make sure to take off my hair tie and my stud earrings, hold my breath and step on making sure that my foot was perfectly even and my weight would be 100 percent accurate.

The days my weight went down, I was elated. I was successful. I hadn't experienced success like this ever before in my life. I was a weight-loss success story. I was somebody and that was new to me. The weeks that the scale didn't move or, Heaven forbid, went up, all of that was stripped away. In my mind, I was a failure. I would be sent back to where I came from—a life of obesity. Back to the "plus size" stores, the judgement for my weight, the constant chafing, the land of not being important. The moment the scale went up, my mind went to war.

After I reached my set goal weight, I was a size two. I had gone from a size twenty-four to a size two. Regardless, I was at the top of what I was taught to be my *healthy range*. I weighed 150 pounds but the way 150 pounds fit my body made me very thin. I was at a point where people who loved me were questioning my health and asking if I was sick or if I was okay.

Even though I was so small and even though I had reached my goal, my unhealthy mind continued to wonder, *What if I just did a little bit more, went a little bit further, took it one level deeper?*

In my obsession to continue to push the limits of my weight loss, I had begun skipping breakfast and seeing how hungry I could get before I *had* to eat. I

145

knew this was tiptoeing in the waters of creating a new ~~eating disorder altogether. I was smart but I was a~~ mess. I was conscious enough not to go too far but confused enough to test the waters. I was destroying the same body that I had set out to make healthy and it was due to never fueling my mind along the way. My mind never came for the ride. I had learned to lose weight—that's it. I had not taken the time or made the effort to become a healthy person.

In preparing to write this book, I looked back on this season of my life in a deep way. I had journaled during this time and the journal was tucked away with my things along with memories of my dad and other pieces of life that I didn't necessarily want to throw away but I wasn't ready to see regularly. It had been five years since I reached my goal weight and I hadn't opened this journal since I wrote in it back then.

I was shocked to read what I found. I knew I was in a bad place but the pain of how bad it was didn't feel so raw. As I read these entries, I shed tears crying over the fact that nobody knew how badly I was suffering. I was putting on face every day to go spread a positive message but on the inside, I was dying. I was crumbling. I sent pictures of these entries to my sister-in-law who has always been my right-hand man on this journey. Her response was with tears, stating that she had no idea. Nobody did.

Keep in mind that at the time of these entries, I had lost 90-100 pounds already and was wearing a size 2/4.

December 10, 2011

"I really battle with the old fat Krystle in my mind all of the time. For example, I gained weight this week and I had a really on plan and physically active

147

week. So, immediately *Fat Krystle* started to wonder why I bother working so hard. *Fat Krystle* is stupid. Then, my mentor told me that I should try to eat my activity calories and my weekly allowance for extras, which is a logical recommendation. *Fat Krystle* hears: 'Eat more food.' So I ended up eating more today, especially at a Christmas party that I attended and not tracking any of it. UGH! Why? Now, I don't even have weekly allowance left. I just wish that this wasn't such a constant battle. I know that the struggle makes it worth it in the end but since there is no real end of this, it's going to be a *lifelong battle.* That makes me... I don't know... I'm rambling..."

April 2, 2012

"I feel fat right now. I don't understand how my body can change so much on a day to day basis. I can look in the mirror and see a different body than the one I saw the day before. I feel like I eat too much. Even though I track it and I have room for it in my plan, lately I feel like I can't stop eating. Then on the flip side, I feel so in control today because I was able to tame my snacking. I have 2,019 followers on my Facebook page who think I am freakin' fantastic. I always share my struggles with them as well as my victories and it seems to draw everybody in... Why do I say all these positive things then come in here and bitch about myself? I guess it's my outlet. *Blah.*

April 21, 2012

"I am disgusted with myself. Last weekend we went away and I ate like complete shit. This week I gained 1.4 pounds but instead of getting back on track, I stuffed my face today... So on top of that, I am eating my emotions. I didn't do it too much the past week but today I stuffed my face. I feel so gross. I have a four-month-old food baby in my stomach and it's absolutely disgusting."

May 30, 2012

"I am tired of talking about watching my weight, which is why I am taking a break from being *Skinny Jeans Dreams* [my Facebook page that tracked my weight loss] for a little while. That page can seriously wear me out some days. There are so many criticizing attitudes and questions sometimes that it drives me nuts. This is a shame. I am sitting here thinking what else to write about and weight loss is all I think about."

October 14, 2012

"I quit working for [insert weight loss company]. I hid the scale in the closet. I just want to LIVE. Right now I feel fat and disgusting after eating pizza and Chinese food today but that's irrelevant. I have been feeling great and healthy lately so that's good. Shit…I'm tired."

October 19, 2012

"I woke up this morning in somewhat of a dark place but self-aware enough to know I was there. I was stressed out about money, Nick, and life in general. My instant *solution* was 'Lose weight. Eat less. Move more.' Despite the fact that none of my problems involved being overweight. A while back I had been binging pretty often and many times I found myself in the bathroom, holding my *pregnant* (food baby) stomach contemplating sticking my finger down my throat. The only thing stopping me then was Elliana and not wanting to start another unhealthy habit…well, and the fact that it didn't work on my first measly attempt. Okay so, I tried. This morning, if I hadn't read

151

my new incredible friend, Nicole's blog post, I would have probably continued with my original solution. I probably would have tried to see how long I could go without needing to eat. Thank God for Nicole. I think she is exactly what I needed to keep me from trading in one obsession for another. I talked to my mom for a while and I am ready to go to a therapist so I can really get to the root of my problems. I think I am scared of what I might learn."

November 14, 2012

"I have issues. I really need to get therapy. So, I hurt my back pretty badly and I haven't been able to work out the last few days but I also haven't been able to slow my eating. During the day, I have been fine but 3:00 pm hits and I can't stop. I stop tracking anything that I had been tracking and pick while I cook, eat, and clean up. Then I am full and regretful. I went back to tracking today since I can't work out. Of course, I went over and felt guilty but I look at what I ate today and I am confused by why I feel any regret at all. I had a banana, rice cakes, a nutritious shake, a slice of an apple, yogurt, strawberries, a VitaTop egg sandwich, mixed veggies, egg whites, a bite of a plum, a bite of an apple, and a kid-sized bag of pretzels. I am lying here feeling fat. Of all things to feel, I feel fat. I hate how powerful my mind can be. I am not fat. My stomach feels flabby since I haven't been able to work out and I look at it and I see fat. How ridiculous am I?! I'm struggling tonight. Like I said—I need help."

My breaking point

Christmas season of 2012. I was sitting on my mom's couch in my size two jeans. What should have been the happiest time of my life was when I found myself at my worst. I was talking with my mom and I

153

picked up a family magazine from the TV stand. On the cover were sweets, treats, and desserts for Christmas and when I looked at it, I began to cry. I cried because the mere thought of being surrounded by sweets and Christmas treats scared me, overwhelmed me, and pushed me to the point of anxiety that I had never experienced prior to this season of my life.

The thought of food scared me. The idea of gaining weight overwhelmed me. This couldn't possibly be how I was supposed to live. It was in that moment that I somehow found my *why* again. I had begun this journey to live healthier for my daughter and yet in the process, I lost sight of that. I was now living a life that was not my own. I was racing against people I didn't know. I was living a lifestyle that I never desired in my heart but somehow, I was there and I was absolutely miserable. Not only was I miserable but I was so mentally unhealthy that what was intended to be good for my family became toxic for them. I was so obsessed with what I put into my mouth, how many calories I burned, what size I wore, how much I weighed, that I was creating a toxic environment not just for myself but for my daughter.

I thought I only mattered if I was losing weight. That became my identity and I no longer knew how to be anything else. It was what I knew how to be successful at when I was never successful at anything else. Until it broke me.

It was in that brokenness that I began to find my truth. As I pieced it back together, I found my voice. But first, it was time to adjust. Actually, it was entirely way past the time I should have adjusted but we learn from our mistakes. We fail and we get back up. Failure, while it hurts, is part of learning what works and what doesn't. I hope that my story can help you avoid some of the painful things I went through to get to where I am today. I hope that if nothing else, it will instill a sense of awareness in you that will help you to know when it's time to adjust your sails.

You see, struggle doesn't discriminate based on your size, your family, your social status. Struggle comes in all shapes and sizes. These things led me to a place where I began to see a therapist. I didn't want to live this way. See, what they don't tell you when you begin a physical transformation journey is that your mind needs to come along for the ride. Your mind needs to transform as well. When you begin to put focus on your body in a way that you never have before, your mind can either be your own best friend or your own worst enemy.

The numbers can consume you. Whether you want to lose 100 pounds or gain twenty pounds, the numbers can consume you if you let them. So, my story continued and through counseling and self-

156

reflection, what made the most sense for me in that season was to give up the numbers. I stopped counting everything. I ditched all of the numbers including the scale until I could get myself on solid ground. That resulted in a thirty-pound weight gain that truthfully saved my life. One might see a thirty-pound weight gain as a terrible problem to have. I see it as the gain that gave me my life back and allowed me to begin to see clearly, in balance, and understand what a life of wellness really could be.

As I experienced this, I began to realize that my story wasn't about weight loss at all. That was just the beginning—just a piece of the puzzle. The rest was about to unfold and my purpose was about to become bigger than inspiring people to lose weight. I could do that; losing weight had become my thing. In my heart of hearts though, I knew there was more.

As the story continued, I recommitted to fitness in a different mindset only to find myself pregnant with my son just a few months later. That brought on an opportunity to truly fall in love with my body in a whole new way. This pregnancy was different. This time, I was fit and strong and had been through this huge physical transformation and now as I began to love the mental growth I was experiencing, I admired my body.

Gaining weight through pregnancy was something I enjoyed. I loved to see my body change day by day as I grew human life and through this process, I became infatuated with the strength and endurance of a woman's body and the ability of it to transform in so many beautiful ways. Learning to love where I was at in this season was healing in more ways than I am sure I could ever put into words.

This part of my story was in place for more than making me a mother again. This part of my story opened up doors to truly connect with myself and with others in a way that I hadn't been able to before. I spent my pregnancy learning to love and embrace my body in each moment. My pregnancy with Maceo healed so many levels for me from a mental perspective.

So here I am looking at thirty, about to enter into marriage, and with a daughter who is now old enough to really know what's going on and internalize the things she hears me say and sees me do. I have tried it all, experienced all sides of failure, picked up the pieces and I'll be straight with you—writing this chapter of the book is my way of releasing this chapter of my life. As I write these words on paper, I am freeing myself wholly and fearlessly from the diet era of my life. It was both purposeful and necessary and now it is my time to move on to the next chapter of my story because my story is about more than how much I weigh. The weight was just this chapter.

I've put in the work and I've pieced together what I know works and what doesn't for my personal life and wellbeing, my body, and my family. My only *plan* at this point is to just live it out. To live authentically in a way that makes sense not just for my body but also for my mind. To be frank, I am tired of talking about diets so much! I've been talking about diets since I was a pre-teen and I am tired. I have no desire to be counting food forever or still trying to figure out what works in another ten years. I want to live. Boldly, freely, wholly in a healthy and well-balanced way.

My beautiful Elliana. My daughter was and still is my inspiration. Being her mom changed me in ways I could never adequately put into words. Both of my children inspire me to be better every day, and every decision I make takes into consideration the effect it will have on them and the legacy it will leave for them. I do not want my kids' memories of childhood to be laced with memories of what diet I was on or how much I talked about weight, food, and diet plans. I want them to remember that I took care of my body, exercised because I love myself, and led by example for them. That's the legacy I want to leave.

That's been the struggle that consumed over twenty years of my life. Over the last several years, I have been able to use my story to bless the lives of others and as I step into my next decade, I will take the good and leave the bad. I will take with me the lessons I have learned that have made me better and continue to write my story. I don't know what lies ahead, but I know that everything we go through in life is a chapter in our book. There are a whole lot of people who need your story to know that they're not alone. Together we

are better.

H: Heal Your Mind

Breathe deeply
Take it all in.
This is your life.
It's yours to live freely.
Healing begins within
Let it course your veins
Traverse your brain
Let it fill you up
Until you're not the same
Let it fill your soul
And nourish your spirit
Like finger paint for your life
Get in there and smear it
Spread it high
And spread it low
Make it beautiful
Make it grow

It's uniquely yours
Take it fast or take it slow
The same wounded warrior
Just wanting to stay alive
Can be the same overcomer
Living a life that thrives
By Krystle J Bailey

We all have scars. We all have battle wounds from the journey of life. All of us have been through something, overcome things, powered through, and seen highs and lows. We all have baggage that we have held on to for far too long.

Believing that we are worthy, enough, beautiful, powerful, and capable of infinite possibilities doesn't come easily for the majority of us. Most of us need to fuel, heal, and nurture our minds daily to really find that core belief that takes you from surviving to thriving. Everything we aspire to do and all that we

164

dream of becoming in life can be achieved through the power of your mind.

But just fueling your mind without healing it is like putting a Band-Aid on a bullet wound. A hurt football player must be healed before he can get back in the game; otherwise the wounds will compound and he will find himself sidelined indefinitely. Healing is a critical part of wellbeing and it takes time, love, grace, and compassion inwardly. The gentle care and love we give our children when they are hurt is the same love we have to show ourselves when it comes to healing our hearts and our minds. Don't we deserve that same kind of gentleness and comfort?

I'm not a doctor so I won't pretend to know anything other than what I know based on my own experiences. My mom often asks me if I wear myself out in my own head. My mind is overactive. The best way I can explain how my mind works ninety-nine percent of the time is like a Chrome browser open with 47.5 tabs open at the same time. That's how I function by nature but when it comes to healing, I must close out a few tabs and focus on the things that need my attention and spend quality time with myself on the things that matter. I've shared with you the power of meditation, prayer, and self-reflection.

I haven't yet shared about the value of personal growth and development and what it has done for my life. I joke about Tony Robbins and speaking things into existence but the reality is that people like Tony Robbins and John Maxwell along with many other motivational speakers and authors have really brought to light an area of living that I hadn't experienced prior to hitting my new rock bottom in 2012. Personal development opened a whole new world for me in ways I never imagined.

I waited entirely too long to begin nourishing my mind. I thought I had it all figured out. I was a young twenty-something-year-old, graduated from college, lost one hundred pounds, was raising a beautiful little girl. The world could not tell me a thing that I didn't already know. I thought I was God's gift to earth. In my story about my weight, it is evident that I was a hot mess.

Truth is, I still am a bit of a hot mess. I think we're all a little bit of a hot mess trying to navigate this *life* thing one moment at a time and being stuck in a world where we are constantly being convinced that we're not enough, that we need to do more and be better. We are in the social media age where images of *perfect* women grace our computer screens and our smartphones every time we scroll Instagram. We see perfect moms, perfect bodies, perfect marriages, perfect kids, perfect, perfect, perfect. And most of us

167

have found ourselves at one point or another comparing our lives to the lives on the screens.

Guess what? They're a hot mess too. We're all just trying to figure this all out. Being a good wife, a good mom, or a good role model doesn't come with handbooks. We're all put on this earth with a purpose and we are given absolutely no hints at figuring out what that purpose is. I'll give you one hint though. Your purpose is not her purpose and her purpose is not yours. Her version of health does not have to mean the same thing for you, nor does her version of happy, her version of balance, her version of fit, or her version of successful. That is for her.

What's for you is waiting for you when you begin to pursue your most authentic self. Your most authentic self is waiting to be explored, to be shared with the world, and to be celebrated but you cannot find her on social media. You cannot find her in the

168

magazines or on TV. You can't find her anywhere except where she's been waiting all along—in you.

When you begin to explore this idea of nourishing and taking care of your mind and begin to pursue what all-around wellbeing feels like, you will begin to uncover that truest you and oh, what a beautiful experience it is. The war that wages in our heads every time we try to be something that we weren't created to be is utterly exhausting and pointless. It's that relentless effort that toddlers make to fit the circle block into the square hole in their toy. It wasn't created to fit and you weren't created to fit the mold of anyone else's life either. As you peel back the layers and fuel your mind, you will begin to see clearly your truth. Living authentically in your truth is an amazing place to live.

In a world when I was becoming *somebody* on social media as I shared my story of weight loss, I thought I had figured out exactly what I was put here for—~~I was going to help people lose weight. That was~~ it, right?! I had nailed my purpose. When I hit that new rock bottom in 2012 on my mom's couch, I had to ask myself—who am I to help anyone?! I need to help myself. And so began my road to personal development.

I loathed those words: Personal Development. I was a new member of a direct sales company that repeatedly told me about the importance of personal development, but I was in denial. Personal development, in my mind, was for people who needed help. *Insert sarcastic tone here:* "I didn't need help. I was the help. I was the hope for people who needed it." Until I ran out and my cup ran dry. I needed to fill my cup if I was ever going to continue to fill the cups of others.

I began reading books, listening to podcasts, watching YouTube videos, attending conferences and I began to yearn for the thirst-quenching refreshment that was personal growth. How had I not known about this before? It was beautiful and delicious and I couldn't get enough. I began to understand what it felt like to not have to pour from an empty cup.

Nourishing my mind meant I could give to others without running myself dry. Nourishing my mind meant I didn't have to run on empty and that I could have purpose, passion, and goals beyond just losing weight. It meant I could learn new perspectives from people all over the world and my scope would begin to be far wider than New Jersey. It meant I could improve in ways that were meaningful and impactful for me on a personal level as well as through business, leadership, communication, and entrepreneurship. It was, and is, the most unexpected and incredible thing

171

that came out of a journey that was originally intended to change the number on the scale.

Personal development changed everything and opened doors of opportunity that I never would have known existed. I am still a part of said direct sales company and do fairly well. However, I stand strong on the fact that if I never made another dime, I would be a better person because of the challenge to grow my mind. Every moment is a steppingstone.

Healing comes when we least expect it. From my story about my dad to the story of seeing a therapist after I lost my weight, through my stories you can see different healing experiences. Some from prayer, others from meditation, while others came through attending seminars or reading books.

Once upon a time I thought that seeking personal growth meant forward motion all of the time. Keep moving forward, keep achieving, keep pursuing.

It wasn't until recently that I've learned to embrace that sometimes personal growth might mean taking a few steps back and taking care of old, useless, self-limiting thoughts so that I can then move forward stronger and more whole than I was prior.

Opening your mind and heart to experience healing is the first step in all of this. If you're not open to it, you'll be hard pressed to experience it. Having wounds that need healing doesn't make you less than enough—it makes you beautifully and wonderfully human. We all carry brokenness in some way or another but we don't have to bear burdens for a lifetime. Healing is calling your name. Take the time to sit with it, embrace it, and nurture it back to health just like you would nurture your son's scraped knee. You're beautiful, scars and all.

Sometimes, even when it stings, the best way to begin healing is for someone we love to hold up a mirror so we can see ourselves from their perspective. Several life changing events that happened in 2012 led to me reversing the ride I was on. The first happened when I was crying over a weight gain one week. Nick, in all his honest advice, told me that I had traded in one unhealthy obsession for another.

At first, his words sent me into a frenzy of anger and frustration. How could he say such a thing when I was working so hard? Of course, I later learned how right he was. It's only in retrospect that I was able to see clearly how obsessive I had become.

The second happened when I met my friend Nicole. She was a fitness instructor with a beautiful body and even more beautiful heart. She had overcome eating disorders of her own and was recovered and living well. Listening to Nicole share her story as well as things she still struggled with was like holding up a mirror to what I couldn't see on my own. It showed me how right Nick was and how deep I had actually fallen.

With Elliana as my continuing driving force, I sobbed big ugly tears at the thought of raising her this way and passing on these demons to her. This whole thing had gotten messy. Sure, I was skinny but I didn't even know myself anymore. I didn't recognize the person staring back at me in the mirror. I didn't know her and I didn't like her. I wanted Krystle—the Krystle I knew and loved back. I wanted to be better. I wanted healing.

I need you to hear me. As I share these things about myself, I want you to hear my heart. Sharing these things is not about me "body shaming" anybody who is currently going through these things or has experienced this. This is real; this was the body shaming and self-hatred that was happening within myself at that time in my life. The same shaming, darkness, and hatred that I know that so many women suffer through in silence. This is me telling you that there is no shame in seeking professional help if you feel out of control. This is me telling you that it is okay and you can heal, you can get better, there is still hope as long as you have air in your lungs. This is me helping to break that silence.

The enemy in your head is a liar. Whatever it is that you're working towards in life, your relentless effort is enough. You are a success because successful people don't quit and you haven't thrown in the towel. They believe in themselves even when the going gets tough. They show up day in and day out, regardless of the outcome.

You are not a failure. I was not a failure. But I wasn't reading a book that helped me change my perspective. I wasn't reading a book that told me the truth: that I was beautiful and the scale could not

176

change that. I was enough and nobody could take that from me. I was loveable because I was God's child and I didn't have to do anything to prove it. I didn't have to lose any more weight to prove that I was worthy of love from others and more specifically, love from myself. I didn't have to show up on Facebook to be important. I already was. I didn't have to prove more results to stay relevant. I was valuable and important because I was Krystle J Bailey and that was enough, but I didn't know that. I didn't feel that. I was at war in my mind until I surrendered that fateful day in 2012 and that is when my healing began.

Strengthening your body is easy. Strengthening your mind is the hard part. The hardest muscle to work is the muscle that lies right between our own two ears. I wish I had a secret sauce, a program, or a shake to help you with that but I don't. Here's what I can tell you:

Just like squats get easier as your legs and glutes get stronger, authentically loving yourself on a deep level gets easier as your mind gets stronger. But it takes time! Not just time but daily work. I've been working on my mind since I hit that new rock bottom in 2012. I've been a work in progress since then and I can honestly tell you that I am at the BEST place I've ever been with myself now in 2017.

For five years I have been actively strengthening my mind and telling myself I was powerful beyond measure, beautiful beyond words, and capable beyond limitations. I've told myself these things even when I didn't fully believe them, just like I work out even when it's not easy. I made a promise to myself that I would keep telling myself these things until I began to believe them because I deserved to truly believe them...because I am a child of the One

True King and I am worthy of believing in my heart of hearts that I AM enough.

Just like some workouts are not too bad and some rock your entire world, I have had good days and bad days on my mental journey but each day I get better. Just as on a physical journey, rest is of utmost importance to the growth and transformation of our minds. Rest and healing are a part of the process. Grow the muscles but don't forget to take a nice hot Epsom salt bath, get a massage, and do some yoga. Your mind works the same way—fill it up with all the good things with personal growth, questions of self-reflection, journaling, therapy, whatever you need to strengthen, but don't forget to let go and just live while you allow yourself to experience the healing. It's easy to get caught in the trap of learning all the time and never living out what you're reading about. Living it out is a part of the healing process.

If I am equating mental fitness to physical fitness, my mind is at a place where it could run an Ironman. Because every. Single. Damn. Day. For four years, I've relentlessly pursued strengthening and healing my mind because I refuse to live in a place where I don't like myself. Because I refuse to accept less than anything than genuine love from the only person who can love me like I can. I refuse to be held back by self-imposed limitations and refuse to believe things that are simply not true about myself. I want to spread my wings and fly and leave all self-doubt, self-hatred, and negativity of the past behind me.

So, my friends, I tell you this to encourage you to keep making promises to yourself, keep working that mental muscle, keep believing in yourself and seeking your own truth, and one day, you'll find a peace that knows no bounds within yourself. You'll find everything you've ever needed right there within you.

It's already there. It's just waiting to be revealed. There is beauty in the healing if you're willing to receive it. The key to seeing your life and experiences in a new way is choosing to change your perspective on the big things as well as the little things.

"Self-love is asking yourself what you need every day and then making sure you receive it."—Unknown

M: Main Thing

Written by my late uncle, Ralph Platt Jr.:

Whether you came to realize it or not, your life is in action.

There are no dress rehearsals and no do-overs. Life is in session. Sometimes people take life for granted. You are only given one life and you have to take advantage of it while you still have the opportunity. Are you just mindlessly going through life without a defined purpose? Just living day to day or week to week trying just to survive? Is your work just a job to pay the bills? Or do you have passion and purpose for your personal and professional life?

Imagine yourself as a much older person. When you reflect back over the course of your life, is the end result a smile or a regret? You are never too old to change, never too old to dream and certainly never too old to begin living your dream.

Stephen Covey famously said, "The main thing is to keep the main thing, the main thing." You might have heard it from Stephen Covey but I learned it from my dear friend, Mikey. Through the years of giving up my body, seeking significance, and figuring out who I was, I met Mikey. In a world where any guy was waiting for a young woman to give herself up in the way that I would, Mikey became a friend. He never took advantage and he listened. He listened to me and challenged me in ways that used to infuriate me when I was young and just wanted him to tell me the answer to his riddles.

Anybody who knows Mikey knows that his Mikey-isms will eventually bless your life but he usually gives them to you in a season of life when you're not trying to hear what he has to say. Like a seed that takes time to grow, it sits and waits. I met

Mikey over ten years ago, at which time he repeated two phrases to me over and over—neither of which made complete sense at seventeen years old. One was, "All things come from within oneself." The other was, "The main thing is to keep the main thing, the main thing."

Certain moments, experiences, and interactions are carried with you for life. These two expressions that were drilled into my head during a confusing time of my life, came along with me for the ride and keeping the main thing, the main thing has saved me in more ways than I can put into words, from my relationship with Nick, to bouncing back in 2012 because of Elliana, to writing this book.

When I realized that this was going to be a chapter in the book, I wrote to Mikey and asked him something I never had before. I asked him, "I know what keeping the main thing the main thing means to

184

me now but can you tell me why it was so important for you to instill in me then?"

His response: "It originally started out as a track mantra. The coach would yell out, *What's the main thing?* and we would yell back, *the main thing is to keep the main thing the main thing.* Coach would then ask *Why?* and we would reply, *because if you listen and apply you can take valuable seconds and hundredths of seconds off your time."* He continued, "I always attempted to look for deeper meaning in the things I did every day. So, I looked into how I could use this mantra as a philosophy to focus on: If perception is reality, I could use the saying to teach others that by prioritizing what is important, you can form a habit and once you form a habit, you can change your very reality. As far as you [me] were concerned, the first thing I wanted you to learn was that your perception was off. That the things you believed were important or the things you felt you needed to be relevant were incorrect and that you were so much more but if you can't see it, you won't be able to project it. Perception may dictate an individual's reality but it does not dictate reality as a whole. For that, we need focus. If we didn't focus on science, we would still believe in magic. If we didn't focus on cultivation, we would still be hunter-gatherers. If we still our focus, maybe one day what is important to us may just become important to the whole world."

You've heard the quote, "Where your mind goes, energy flows," right? My perception of the main thing is just that. What this means to me is keeping in the forefront of my mind what is important, what matters, what I will take with me for life and not just in this season. Simply identified for the context of this book—my priorities: my spiritual, mental, physical, and relational wellbeing. My personal nourishment.

186

The main thing in my life is staying whole and not sacrificing myself, my body, my mind, my relationships, or my peace for anyone.

When I sacrifice my wellness for anybody, the main thing is not intact. That doesn't mean I don't lose sleep sometimes for my kids or sacrifice time to help a friend in need. This is about peace and overall wellbeing. This is sacrificing my marriage for money or sacrificing quality time with my kids for the sake of recognition. It's sacrificing my time with God for things that don't really matter in my life. As much as I love each and every one of my friends, my marriage and my children come first so if those are sacrificed, the main thing remains out of place.

Keeping the main thing, the main thing is about identifying what is the absolute most important in your personal life and keeping it front and center in your life. There are always going to be shiny objects, new opportunities, distractions that will attempt to pull you away from your main thing but your job is to protect it and to focus on it. Put your energy into keeping it where it belongs.

Like anything in life, you're going to have moments where you slip up. You'll lose sight of the main thing, you'll drop the ball on a priority or two but when you have your main thing clearly identified, bolded, italicized, and highlighted, you'll always know how to come back and you won't get too far away from it.

Keeping the main thing, the main thing is harder if you keep that thing to yourself. Tell someone what it is that is important to you. Tell your spouse that you read this chapter and your priorities are X, Y, and Z. Ask for support in keeping them in focus when things get a little wild in life. Creating personal, family, and career mission statements is a great way to keep your main things in focus all of the time. Not only does it help to keep it in focus but it also helps to identify your priorities and usually will open your eyes about a thing or two.

Every time I write a mission statement for a new business or I rewrite one for a new season of life, I am challenged by this question: Do I really live this way? Or am I writing it because it sounds good? I am often challenged to tweak some of the ways I am living to match the way that I desire to live. The process of writing a mission statement is just as important as keeping it in laser focus.

My personal mission is *to fearlessly follow my God-given path and to use my voice to speak light and positivity into the lives of others.*

My personal mission statement is actually relatively new. As I sought out my truth, my mission statement changed. Not long ago, the same personal mission statement had more to do with weight loss and fitness and empowering people's lives through those things. While those things are still important to me, in truth seeking, I learned that my mission and my purpose are much bigger and broader than that. So this personal mission statement now fits the way I live with a more open mind, a broader purpose, and living in my truth.

If you don't already have a personal mission statement, take this time to write one. There is no greater time than the present. Three questions to ask yourself to get you started are, *What value do you create? Who are you creating it for?* and *What is your expected outcome?* A mission statement should be brief—three to five sentences at most. It should get down to the core of what you want out of life and what you represent. Who are you? Think about it as something that will guide your day to day even when your career or your lifestyle changes. What's important to you and what really matters? What will still matter in another ten years? What kind of legacy do you want to leave?

Keep it positive. Try to use positive words and phrases like *I will* and *I am* rather than phrases like *I will never* or *I don't*. These are some tools to help you get started but there is also a world of information out there on the world wide web. Seek out some inspiration and then make it your own. Speak your personal truth into your mission statement.

In the same realm, I also have a family mission statement. I got a little creative on my family mission statement. I kind of have a thing for acronyms and wordplay. To preface this, I have to tell you that my maiden name is Bailey and that is what I use for business purposes. My married name is Turner. My family mission statement spells out Turner.

In this family we:

Trust in God always

Understand and respect each other

Reach out and help one another

Nurture and cherish each moment together

Empower and encourage big dreams and goal chasing

Rise together as a team

All the same things I shared about writing a personal mission statement remain true in writing a family mission statement. This is something we hang in our home and read daily. In creating a family mission statement together and brainstorming as a team, you open yourself up to hearing the priorities of your family in a new perspective, no matter how young or old each member might be.

Let's keep it real though; if you have little kids like me and a husband who is working a lot and leaves most family decisions up to you, you might want to rough draft this family mission statement and then bring it to the table to make things go a little smoother. However you do it, the idea is to put in place a set of guidelines to live by that you keep focused on as the main thing in your home. Will you stray? You betcha! We all have moments where we lose our tempers and fail to respect each other with our words because we're human but having this front and center in your home is a sure way to bring you back to the main things in your life.

Digging a little deeper into keeping the main thing front and center, ask yourself *why*. This is a question I ask myself with every new endeavor and every goal that I set. Why am I doing this? Why does it matter? What purpose does it serve my life? In business, I encourage the women I mentor to have a *why* that makes them cry and keeps them coming even when the going gets tough. My *why* saved me when I was starting out on my weight loss, saved me again when I went too far. My *why* encouraged business growth as well as the opportunity to slow down. My *why* inspires me to leave a legacy and to make an impact.

When I make decisions, they are planted in whether or not they will answer the question *why,* Ninety-nine percent of what I do and why I do it revolves around my family. They're also the reason I won't say yes to certain opportunities that don't align with my priorities. Having a strong and clearly defined reason for all the things you do connects you emotionally and personally and simplifies the idea of keeping focus on those priorities and mission statements.

Keeping the main thing, the main thing is not always as simple as it might seem. Life is going to happen, we're going to stumble and fall, people are going to hurt us, and life is going to take unexpected

194

turns. When you clearly define and constantly remind yourself of what truly matters and you continue to pour love, energy, and focus into those things, you'll always know how to find home base. There is nothing as sweet and as comforting as home base.

E: Empowering Women

Around Us

She looks at herself in the mirror and sighs.

She is deep in the quicksand, believing all of the lies.

What's true and what's not?

She doesn't know anymore.

She was winning these mind games

But now she's lost score.

Every morning she stares at her body

As she picks it apart

She wishes she could remember how she got here

When did this war start?

It's been so long, it's her reality now

She wants to turn back time

But she doesn't know how.

As she steps on the scale,

She lets out a scoff.

"Mommy" she hears, "It's my turn, get off!"

She falls to her knees in tears of guilt.

She hugs her baby girl as she vows to rebuild.

"No, baby. You don't need this

And neither do I."

She finds her worth that morning

In her daughter's eyes.

The eyes that look at her in love and admiration.

The little girl staring back at her

Becomes her biggest motivation.

"Today is the day," she claims,

"That I'll release the weight and the shame.

Today I'll find my worth somewhere else

Like maybe, just maybe, inside of myself."

By Krystle J Bailey

Oh, how excited I am to be here at this chapter.

This, my beautiful friend, is what it's all about for me.

If I kept all of these thoughts and ideas about living a

more balanced and whole life to myself, what good would any of it be? It is not only my joy but it is my responsibility to share this with you and with the world. It is my life's purpose to use my story, my voice, my message to empower and uplift every woman God should see fit for me to inspire. There is nothing I love doing more than empowering women, young women, old women, little girls, baby girls. It brings tears to my eyes when I genuinely look at a woman and tell her how beautiful she is or how much she matters. When I get the opportunity to talk to a woman who hasn't heard words of affirmation spoken to her in such a long time that she doesn't know how to accept my authentic compliment, I want to hug her tight and tell her how truly amazing she is every single day.

Women. Beyonce said it best: *Who runs the world?! Girls!* I never loved being a woman as much as I do in this season of my life. My skin is loose, my breasts are the furthest thing from perky, I have stretch marks and varicose veins, and I look at my body in awe at all that my body can do, the way it nurtured my children, the way it loves my husband, the strength it represents both physically and figuratively.

The power of a woman is beyond words. It is an honor and a joy to be a woman. When I look at my body, I see the mind and the heart that are embodied within it that love so deeply and think so broadly. When I cry, I just let it go and let it flow. I love being a sensitive creature who feels for the stuffed animal that got left behind by my two-year-old because it had sentimental value.

When I am fierce, I can almost literally hear myself *rawr!* When I am sad, I love the taste of my tears and the hug of my own embrace or of someone who loves me. When I am happy, I shout it from the rooftops because I love how much I like to talk. When a friend comes to me with sadness or grief, I hurt for them because empathy is one of the best and most beautiful traits of being a woman. I simply love every single part of being a woman and even more than that, I love helping other women shift their perspectives just enough so that they can embrace all that they are but still allow themselves to be uniquely their own.

To me, nourishing my body has nothing to do with my weight, my jean size, or my biceps. Nourishing my body is about taking care of the heart that loves my husband, the arms that hug my children, the shoulders that my friends lean on, the legs that carry me through life, and the lap that I pray my grandchildren will one day sit on. It's about taking care of my mind, body, and soul in a way that nurtures and nourishes me kindly, gently, and lovingly. It's knowing when to ramp things up and knowing when to slow them down. It is kindness shown to the one person that I am most responsible for – myself.

I spent most of my teenage years, young adult years, and up until I was about twenty-seven figuring out how to like myself. I got better as the years passed, stumbled and fell, picked myself back up and kept on in this pursuit of liking who I am on the inside and out and everywhere in between. I know how hard that road is. I know through my own eyes and through the lenses of the women that I have worked alongside of for several years.

I've worked with women who have physically harmed themselves, struggled with eating disorders, hated who they were as a person and as a mom, and struggled with looking themselves in the eyes. I know and understand the struggle that so many women endure just trying to like who they ar. It's one that I wouldn't wish on my worst enemy. Every one of these

201

women including the woman reading this book are children of God—beautifully and wonderfully made, created in His image. It's easy to say and it's often hard to believe and to embody.

To truly feel and believe in your heart of hearts that you are *enough* is one of the greatest challenges of modern womanhood. We've talked about the comparison game and the mental wars, the social media and the print media constantly telling us that we need to be more.

Honey, I am here to tell you and I will tell you a million times over that you do not need to be fixed. You are not broken. If there is one thing we need to fix as women, it's this false idea that we need to fix anything at all. Who you are is who you were created to be, and who you will become is still left untold but she is enough too.

I know that there is someone in your life who has made you feel otherwise or taught you to believe that this is not true but it is in your power to take back what's yours—to take back the truth that you are beautiful and powerful beyond any measure of words. This is your invitation to take it back. Own it, protect it, embrace it, embody it. You, my beauty, are so special and so unique. You might be struggling right now; hang on. You might not feel these words yet; keep reading them. Say them out loud. Visualize and embody what it feels like to feel like the fierce, powerful, empowered woman that you already are. Let her out. Let her shine!

Now, it's our job, as united women, to empower the next girl. It's our job to pay it forward. Think for a moment if your daughter, your niece, your grandchild, your best friend's daughter could grow up in a world where women not only loved each other but they loved themselves. What if they could grow up in a world where women honored and respected themselves in a natural and authentic way? Not egotistically but in a way that they never had to take back their truths. What if they were raised up in their truth so strongly that nobody could take it away from them to begin with? What if our daughters could carry with them the armor of self-love and respect as they go out into the world?

Are you feeling my dream yet? This is my dream for my baby girl and the next generation of women. If you're sold on the vision, I want to tell you more. Are you ready for this?

It starts with you. It starts with us. We are the women who can make the difference. We can break the cycle of self-hatred and body shaming. So many women all over social media right now are doing their part to spread the self-love message far and wide.

Jump on board! There is enough sunshine for everybody on this boat.

Here's the catch though. It's not about just telling your friends that they're enough, your mom that she is important and valuable, or telling your daughter that she is beautiful. It's about owning within yourself that you are all of those things, first and foremost. It's about owning and embracing the body, mind, and spirit that you have been given and letting your light shine bright into the lives of your friend, mother, and daughter.

My mom dieted the majority of my childhood. She lost a significant amount of weight when I was young, put a lot of it back on, tried different diet plans and went to different meetings—many of which I tagged along at her hip for. My mom did the best that she knew how to do at that time. She didn't know that her dieting and self-image would translate into

205

insecurities of my own. She was doing the best she knew how to do with the resources she had raising kids in the late 1980s and early '90s. My mom was a rock star mom and continues to be, as far as I am concerned. She was and still is my hero so, unknowingly to her, what was okay for her to feel and say about herself became okay for me to feel about myself. Mom, I love you.

When you know more, you do more. I have a daughter now and I have a career in empowering people to live better. I attend self-help seminars and read personal-growth books. I know more than my mom knew in the '90s about the impact our words and actions have on our babies. So as a mom raising a daughter post 2010, it is my responsibility to use what I know to enhance and better my daughter's future. At the end of the day, all that I know and all of the motivational speeches in the world can't change anything until I change myself. I have to look in the mirror and decide to have love and admiration for who I am.

I must choose my faces when my daughter sees me try on a bikini that might not fit. My words that I use regarding myself, the faces that I make when she jiggles my arm, the conversations that I have with other women in front of her all matter. They all matter. They matter more than we think they matter. What we say and what we believe about ourselves, especially out loud but even internally, our kids will see and they will have permission to feel those things about themselves. I am in no way perfect at this and as with all things, a constant work in progress. But I am mindful and I am conscious about the truths I create for my daughter.

If just one woman who is reading this book would pick up what I am putting down and begin to apply it to her life, that's one woman in the right direction of my dream. If she then told her friend about this whole crazy idea from some lady named Krystle, we would be another step in the right direction. If my dream became our dream and we began to band together to first love and empower ourselves and then each other, just think about the impact we could have on the women who will carry on our legacy.

You know what's most amazing to me out of all of this? It's that my mom now looks to *me* for self-empowerment. She comes to me when she feels overwhelmed with food or negative self-talk. She asks me for advice when she is struggling because she trusts me to guide her. She now minds her words in front of my babies, her grandchildren, because she knows the value of words and the impact they hold. She taught me more lessons in life than I could ever repay her for but it is my life's greatest joy to have been given a voice that empowers not just my daughter but my mother. It's full-circle validation of what I've been put on this earth for.

I don't want to just stop with my mom and my daughter though. I want this vision to spread. I don't care where you hear it from, whether it be me, Ashley Graham, Chalene Johnson, or some other motivational woman in your world. If we could spread this vision, these words, this shift in thinking to every woman we know, I would bet my life that the next generation of women would be so much more enlightened and empowered than we were.

Look, I am not doctor or psychologist. I've never spent sleepless hours reading a psychology book or with my nose buried in some research study. I hate studying now. I told you this earlier in the book—all I know is what I know. I know my own experiences and how they have impacted my life. I think outside of the

box and seek the bigger picture in life. I am a woman
raised by women, raising a young woman, surrounded
by other women in my career and in life. And I think
that together, we can do so much better.

The following paragraphs are stories told by
two of my friends and women that I have had the
pleasure of experiencing life with. Tameka and Kerri
both have shared in similar experiences growing up. I
share these stories delicately and with love, as just as
my mom did her personal best, the mothers of Tameka
and Kerri did as well. These two stories are two of
many that I have heard over the years. Our words
matter more than we realize!

Tameka's story

I remember my mother telling of being in third
grade, weighing 103 pounds, and her mother putting

her on a diet. My grandmother, with good intentions I am sure, never stopped urging my mother to lose weight as a child or an adult.

As I started gaining weight in childhood my grandmother would remind me of how "chubby" I was getting over the years. My mother did not skip a beat in coming to my rescue during these times and would not allow any negative talk about my weight. My mother was able to recognize the obvious ways these negative words would impact me, but it was the things that would happen over the next several years that would impact me most.

For as long as I can remember my mother was always trying to lose weight. Always saying she wished she could lose x number of pounds. She would try on clothes in the dressing room and touch her stomach and say she looked pregnant or complain of her "thunder thighs". I never remember a time where she truly felt like she was enough and liked her body.

It was these moments that showed and taught me as a growing child that this is how women were. That we see the reflection of our bodies and allow that reflection to determine the words we say and thus determine the way we feel about ourselves. That we either had the "ideal body type" or were trying to lose weight, and that there was nothing in between.

Kerri's story

"Fat."

"Size doesn't matter."

"Ugly."

"You're beautiful the way you are."

"Overweight."

"Big boned."

"I ate too much."

212

"Eat more."

These are the conflicting expressions of my childhood. I was blessed to have loving, supportive parents who provided all that we needed and then some. Unfortunately, my parents did not model or teach healthy habits. I'm not just talking about what foods are healthy and what portions are appropriate. What I really mean is that they regularly and often threw around negative self-talk. The tiny, self-deprecating daggers started cutting a hole in my heart.

How could the people I loved the most see themselves in such a self-deprecating light? Why didn't they see how wonderful they truly were? As a child, trying to reconcile your thoughts with your parents' words is bewildering. I just saw my parents as amazing people; I didn't measure them by their numbers on the scale or by the portions on their plate.

213

Rather, I thought of their crazy (albeit embarrassing) cheers at my volleyball games, the personal chauffeuring to my litany of obligations and extracurriculars, their hugs and encouragement.

But then, as I got older, I really started to reflect on the juxtaposition between the way my parents put themselves down and the way they lifted us up. As a child, I was never obese, but eventually as a teenager my poor eating habits overtook my physical activity/calorie burning at dance and volleyball. My parents always endeavored to tell me that my size didn't define me and that I was just "big-boned."

My father especially reminded me how beautiful I was on a regular basis. But it was really hard to hear these positive comments and truly internalize them when all I was hearing was my own mother put herself down about her weight, appearance, eating habits, and much more. I think when I was sixteen I stopped believing my parents. I stopped feeling like I was perfect the way I was, and started seeing my deficiencies. The size of my pants was too big, my shirts too tight, my breasts oversized, my food portions too large, my body not attractive. I started wondering if anyone could love a girl like me.

These are just two stories of women who have been through similar experiences. I am not here to tell you how to parent or what you've done wrong. You haven't done anything wrong and neither did your mother. I am only here to encourage you to think about *what if?* What if you could make a better impact? What if you could begin to believe these positive affirmations you're telling yourself? What if the little girls in your life never had stories like mine, Tameka's, Kerri's or countless other women struggling with their self-image? What if we lived in a world where women naturally and authentically empowered and believed in

one another?

I might be wrong.

But what if I'm right?

N: Nurturing Relationships

"Therefore, as God's chosen people, holy and dearly loved, clothe yourselves with compassion, kindness, humility, gentleness, and patience. Bear with each other and forgive one another if any of you has a grievance against someone. Forgive as the Lord forgave you. And over all these virtues put on love, which binds them all together in perfect unity."
Colossians 3:12-14 NIV

Slow down and look up

How often do you rush, rush, rush and go go go and miss the little moments of life? I know I am incredibly guilty of this especially when I am trying to get kids to and from school and activities, cook dinner, finish my work for the day, and still have time to take a breath.

I am always rushing—not just myself but my children. Recently I was giving my daughter a bath and she asked me, *Mommy does this bath have to be a fast one or can I play?* Insert sound of my heart breaking. Of course, with tears of guilt, I told her that she could play and didn't have to rush as I quietly whispered to myself to slow down and not miss the moments, as they all too quickly turn into memories.

Life is full of those constant reminders to slow down, to pay attention, and to look up. I have been guilty for a long time of being tied to my phone or computer for work while my kids are there playing and asking for my attention. *One more minute,* I would reply, which inevitably turned into five more minutes. My daughter is old enough now to quickly correct me these days. She will count to sixty and tell me when my time is up before I have time to argue. Truth is, I couldn't be more thankful for her. She's right. One minute of me being tied to my phone is one minute with my children that I can't get back.

I've spent the last several years being consumed by technology. I have been a work-at-home, hustling momma for several years in different capacities, working to make a name for myself online. Answering my phone with every ring, ding, and beep has been the norm for my life.

Recently, I've been challenging that norm and leaving my phone behind when we go places or plugged in in the bathroom while I am with my family. Every night I've been putting the phone away and just watching my kids put on shows, talking to my husband and looking him in the eye, going on walks together without having to check my text messages first, snagging every tickle that I can get because I'm not missing moments while my head is in my phone.

It's not just with my children though. It's when I am with my family for my grandmother's birthday or at a girls' night out that I have been checking every five minutes, or less, to make sure I haven't missed that precious high of a Facebook *like*.

This past summer, I was hanging out with a couple of friends having some drinks after the kids fell asleep. We were sitting outside talking about life, business, parenting, you name it. My friend Leah called me on my habits. She was sharing something with me about her new relationship and I glanced down to check the text that just came in while she was speaking. She stopped her conversation and said, "Krystle, I love you but one of my biggest pet peeves in life is when I am having a conversation with someone and they're in their phone." *Ouch.*

220

It's been almost a year since she said that to me and I still carry it with me when I am having a conversation with a friend. I wonder how many other people feel that way but aren't gutsy enough to say that that makes them feel less than important? I know I want to be looked at when I am speaking to someone so who am I to not give that same level of respect? I'm working on that balance to date.

As an entrepreneur with business running through your devices, it's a challenge but what I am learning more and more, as I connect deeper with my truth, is that my in-person relationships matter exponentially more than the majority of *friends* on Facebook. The people who want my help in fitness or business will still be there when I go back to my computer later, but the relationships I have in person might not if I don't nurture them.

This past year has been a world of shifts for me, as I continue to grow and learn about what truly makes me happy in life and go after it. This area of looking up is just another one of those areas of growth that I have had to struggle with to see the value and the beauty on the other side of the coin. For years I have built my persona and reputation on Facebook and while it's still important to me, it's much more important to build and nurture the relationships that are still there after I close my screen.

I've hustled for years. I've worked day and night for goals I thought were meant for me because someone else told me the only way to achieve success was to hustle all of the time and sacrifice a little now for a lot later. That made sense until my sacrificing a little became sacrificing too much and the *a lot* part of this deal wasn't happening for me. With priorities in line and the promise of grand amounts of income not knocking down my door, I had to scale myself back to the things that really matter.

My kids are getting older and wiser before my eyes, and there are moments that I will never get if I don't catch them now. I've invited myself to just slow down in all areas of my life including the need to be "on" all of the time. Because I live in my truth now, I didn't need permission from anybody else to do so.

People love you for who you are, not what you do:

They say you're like the five people you spend the most time with. Well, if that's the case, I am more than okay being like Lauren, Tamara, Lexi, Morgan, and Tierra. Those are my best friends and each of those friendships look a little different but each of them is full of love, respect, and admiration for each other. Some of them I talk to every day while others I talk to once a month or once a week but each one of those

relationships is invaluable and irreplaceable to me.

Lauren has taught me a great deal about friendship and what nurturing relationships look like. She is the most nurturing and welcoming person I have ever met. She comes to your house with gifts; you go to her house and she has gifts. She comes to my house, and I say *Let's order Mexican tonight.* I go to her house, and she has a full course meal prepared and a glass of wine poured. I never had a friend like Lauren so when we first fell into this place where I began to consider her a great friend and then one of my best, I started to feel like maybe I wasn't doing enough to be hospitable when she came to visit.

She lives a few states away so the drive to each other is usually about six or seven hours, depending on New York City traffic. What I've learned over the years is that who Lauren is and who I am are two very different people who find common ground, and that is what true friendship is about—accepting and loving all of the other person for exactly who they are.

Lauren's take:

"I'm going to make you the best vegan tacos ever. I found a recipe on Pinterest. I'm so excited, I even got Bill and Nick steak to grill for theirs. I can't wait till you get here so hurry up and drive faster'

After a five-hour drive from Connecticut to a blueberry-loving town in New Jersey, we pull into Krystle and Nick's road, cute little houses and manicured lawns all in a row. Very different from the view you get pulling into my driveway. In my town your neighbors are cows and tractors and your own back yard is a pasture for horses. We are country.

After a long day of travel and highways it's so nice to know we will be spending our New Year's Eve weekend celebrating with some of our favorite people.

The perfect way to end an amazing year. Excited is an understatement when I am able to see my best friend after a few months apart even though we talk every day, video chat, text, and use a walkie-talkie app, but nothing compares to what seeing each other in person does for our souls after a long stint of just virtual hugs.

We grab our stuff from the trunk of the car and head to the door. We don't even knock and there Krystle is beautiful as always with her arms open wide and two of my favorite little ones at her feet waiting to give us big hugs.

Seconds after we exchange hellos, she proclaims with a deep sigh, "I'm so sorry, I forgot to turn the crockpot on and that amazing dinner I planned is ruined, my house is a mess and I just couldn't find my life today, I know you would have had a huge meal ready and every comfort of home waiting for us but thank you for loving me as I am."

I laugh and say with true meaning it's no big deal. After some teasing from Bill and reassurance from me encouraging her that it's really okay, we do what we always do - we talk about where to eat or running to the little Italian store up the road to grab something to cook. As always, we settle on this amazing Mexican place just a mile or so away, where we bring our own tequila, sit at our favorite table and watch Maceo eat the restaurant out of bean dip.

We laugh, probably tear up a little... So far in this book I'm sure you've heard Krystle say she cries ALOT... We are criers. Happy or sad, we cry. Together we are relaxed. Together unfiltered and unedited. Most importantly unconditional. Unconditional love—accepting someone for who they are, knowing they are enough and ultimately forgiving

227

their transgressions. After all it's not our place to judge. That's how I love, it's how I was raised and it's just what I do.

The time spent at the Turners is always welcoming, fun and uplifting even when the guest/kids shower doesn't work and my six-foot-something husband is taking a bath with plastic octopuses and sail boats...judgement free of course. Unconditional friendship. I don't love Krystle more because she's an amazing cook, has a super clean house, warm fluffy towels waiting for post shower. I love Krystle because she makes me a better me, she challenges my spirit and she calms my inner voices. She completes a piece of me that I never knew I needed. She loves me FOR ME.

Me...

Who just happens to LOVE to entertain others, cook large meals, decorate, clean and bring the comfort of home to my guests. Our friends tease me

228

about being the Martha Stewart of the group – "Just ask Lauren, she will know how to make that, fix that, understand that. She knows the most random things."

That's me though, someone who was raised to feed, nourish and love on people with actions and apparently have the brain of an elephant. When I have company coming from out of town or down the street, I will spend days planning a meal, scrubbing the house, setting the perfect dining room table layout, shopping for comfort foods, buying little gifts and making my home theirs. I love, loving on others. It's what my mom does. It's what my grandmother did and it's just what I know.

You couldn't walk into my grandmother's house without having a snack aka a seven-course Italian meal tied to her southern roots with a batch of fried chicken and white gravy. You left full and you left loved. It's just ingrained in me to want others to feel

229

that comfort that brought me so much peace in a chaotic childhood. I don't do for others, expecting grand gestures in return. I do it because that's who I am. So when I do come over, I don't expect a home-cooked meal or a Stepford welcome and a red carpet. What I want is time and what she gives is a judgement-free zone that will most likely include a bottle of wine for her, vodka for me, unplugged conversation and the comfort of knowing that who I am is enough

That's all I need and that's exactly what Krystle brings to the table for me that makes her such an amazing friend and sister. That to her I am enough in all that I am and all that I do. And I know she feels the same about me.

That is the greatest part about real, authentic, relationships and nurturing them in ways that fuel and inspire them to grow. Morgan, Tamara, Lexi, Tierra and I all have different relationships, different ways of serving and loving on each other, different ways we understand each other and communicate with one another. But what all of these relationships have is love and respect and mutual effort to bring out the best in each other. To me, that's what nurturing relationships is—bringing out the best in the other person and loving them fiercely even when they're at their worst.

My sister and I have necklaces that we have had for years. We got them when I was eighteen years old and she was fourteen. They have a picture of the two of us and on the other side, they say, "Never look down on a sister except to pick her up." This is not only how I treat my biological sister but all of these women I consider my sisters. We are the tide that raises all ships.

Good relationships with others begin with a good relationship with yourself

"If you put a small value on yourself, rest assured that the world will not raise your price."—Author Unknown

From my marriage to my friendships to business contacts, even how I talk to my mother, my relationships improved as I improved. As I learned to truly love who I am, I began to learn what it looked like to truly love others free of judgement and with an open and empathetic heart. Removing the self-critiquing judgement that I was imploding upon myself allowed me to see others in a more positive light also. Doing so also allowed me to raise my standard on how I would accept to be treated.

I am a lover and an includer and I am quick to call someone a friend or tell them I love them. In doing

232

so, I've had some pretty crappy relationships over the years. I've accepted verbal abuse from people out of fear of them talking negatively about me to others. I have held on to bad romantic relationships knowing that he was seeing another woman at the same time because I longed to feel important and accepted even if it killed my heart. I hardly stood up for myself and typically let people take advantage of me without giving anything in return. If I wanted someone's love and acceptance, I would bend over backwards to get it, even put myself in danger to achieve it. What I would get in return was minimal compared to the effort I put out to please people.

A funny thing happens when you begin to respect yourself though. When you begin to show yourself love and appreciation and seek God's approval over man's. Suddenly, the bar that you set for how you're treated begins to rise. You begin to say *no* to the things that don't align with your priorities. You begin to treat people with kindness in a different way, in a way that doesn't mean you have to sacrifice yourself or your wellbeing to respect them. You begin to see the best in people because you see the best in yourself and this alone can change the entire dynamic of any relationship. Not only do you begin to raise your bar but you begin to raise the bar for others as well and meet them where they're at.

I am very mindful of where my energy goes. Learning to love and respect myself meant that I didn't need everyone to love me anymore. I didn't need to be validated or accepted by everybody I do life with. So now, I choose my relationships wisely and am conscious of where my energy is placed. I am also cautious about the energy that I receive from others. I choose to surround myself with people who speak life and positivity, and I keep my distance from those who suck the life out of me. Protecting yourself and your peace doesn't make you a heartless or cold person. It gives you the ability to give the best of yourself to the right people and to preserve your energy, your light, your love for the people you are meant to be pouring into. I find nothing wrong with stepping away from someone who maybe you thought you would be friends with but it didn't quite go as planned.

When it comes to setting relationship standards, I always like to joke with my good friend, Morgan. She is the queen of setting her friendship bar from the beginning. I met Morgan at a group play date shortly after we both had our babies. We quickly connected, as our babies were two days apart. For several weeks, we would meet at the playdates and talk about how we should get together outside, go for a run, take the kids to the park, or have a glass of wine together.

When I first reached out to Morgan via Facebook, she had seen that I was hustling fitness programs at the time and she said, "I am interested in what you have to offer but I need to know you're my friend before anything else." Noted.

A few weeks later we finally were planning to hang out together and she told me in her very matter of fact but loving voice, "I have enough flaky friends. I'm looking for friends who are going to show up for life with me, just so you know."

Morgan and I have been best friends now for over two years and we spend countless weekday hours keeping each other company, leaning on each other, and raising our little ones together. While many people may have been taken back by Morgan and her matter of fact statements on what she wanted in a friend, I was inspired by it and I respected her for it. I met her where she was at and I was blessed with one of the most loyal friends I've ever known.

Relationships. They're one of my top four priorities of a well-nourished life. We were not created to do life alone and sure, while relationships come and go, I thrive on the good, solid, nurturing relationships that I hold close to my heart. When these ties are well, it is a crucial piece to my overall wellbeing. The worst punishment in the world for me would be solitary confinement. I am a people person and as I grow into who I was created to be, the people who surround me are the cream of the crop. I am truly blessed by the people who are in my circle and I couldn't fathom ever doing life without them.

Make time for the people you love. Choose your circle wisely. Your vibe attracts your tribe. Protect your energy and raise your bar. Meet people where they're at. Love the best way that you know how and accept that someone else's best way might

look a little different. Relationships are the spice of life

and I like my life eclectic.

T: Trust the Journey

I have this tattooed on my collarbone: *Trust the Journey*. I got the tattoo when I had lost all of my weight and the real internal struggles were taking center stage. I was lost in so many ways and yet figuring out this new life I had created for myself. I didn't know quite where I was and I didn't know where I'd be going from there but deep down, I knew that there was always tomorrow. I always knew that tomorrow would bring new hope, new grace, new mercies, and sometimes it took a lot of tomorrows to get there. I didn't know where my life would head from that point on but I knew I had to hang on. I knew

I had to trust the journey and allow my life to unfold as it would.

A journey of any kind starts with so much unknown. Whether we are setting out to lose weight, change our habits, build a new career, enter into marriage, or become parents, the list of unknowns far outweigh what we know as we go into it. All we know is that we desire these things for our life and that we've been led to this point. I've been on many of these paths, from becoming a young mom to losing a significant amount of weight to building businesses.

I've failed. A lot. I struggle and often have to take things back to my truth, my core self, and meditation to figure out my next step. All too often, I try to do it without prayer or meditation and fall flat on my face in the process. I've been depressed and anxious on my bedroom floor and settled, content and happy in my purpose. I've been a size twenty-four;

I've been a size two and everywhere in between. I've built and rebuilt businesses as many times as necessary. I've struggled in my relationship in ways that should have broken people. I've apologized to my children for my actions and my choice of words more often than I care to admit. I have restarted the writing of this book at least ten times. You might be wondering why am I so happy and fulfilled in life if I am such a work in progress all of the time. Because I've learned to trust the journey. I've learned that I won't always know what tomorrow brings but I can make the most of today.

It comes down to two simple things for me. These two things see me through every season, in every area of life, and keep me coming back for more. They're my golden keys to living a life of wellness and self-love. They've become sort of friends to me. They're kind of like my proverbial angel and devil on

241

my shoulders, except they're both good. There's no room for the devil in my life to even get close to my shoulders so I choose two angels. These two things are: Balance and Grace.

Balance, she likes to test her limits. She likes to challenge me and see how far I can go before it's time to swing the pendulum back the other way. She shows me that I can have fun and live life out loud but that it's still important to slow down, reflect, and reel things in. She keeps my feet on solid ground when the winds of life are blowing around me, and she reminds me to move like a palm tree, to bend but never break.

Balance reminds me that wine with my girlfriends is a form of bonding, not cheating on my diet. She also reminds me that the word *diet* sucks and if we would all just listen to her a little more, we wouldn't need diets. Balance reminds me to turn the technology off and be present in my real world and

242

that the social media world will still be there tomorrow—those things actually don't go away.

Balance is vacations without a care in the world, hustle mode when I come home. Balance challenges me to think about the things that actually matter and say no to the things that don't. She reminds me that I will always stay on solid ground when I pursue my priorities first. Balance is a great *angel* to have hanging around.

On my other shoulder, there's Grace. Grace is so gentle and kind. She reminds me daily that I am God's child, created in His image. She sits with me each morning as I pray that today I could be a better mom, pay better attention to how I fuel my body, keep up with my roles in life. Grace is always there with me and God and my coffee in the morning and pops her head in throughout the day to make sure I know she's still around. She agrees that the laundry isn't that serious and I'm still a good wife whether or not my husband's shirts are hung. She likes macaroni and cheese on the floor because she knows my kids are growing so quickly, messes won't last forever.

She tells me it's okay to be a work in progress and there is nothing wrong with failure as long as I keep moving forward. She reminds me that it's not really failing until I actually throw in the towel and quit and that she is needed for this ride of life. She pats me on the back and tells me to keep going and reminds me that whatever happens, she will be there. She's sent to me from God and as long as I have faith in her, she will have faith in me.

Balance and Grace. That's how I get through each season of my life, no matter what life throws at me. They are the glue that holds together the first ten principles I shared with you. Without Balance, I am all over the place and out of connection with myself.

Without Grace, I am nothing. I playfully personified Grace but the truth is, it's God's grace that has gotten me through it all and to this place. It's God's grace that has allowed us to take where I've been and create this moment together. It's God's grace that will continue to carry me through to what's yet to come and something tells me, there's more where this came from.

Whatever season of life, of love, of hardship or victory you may be in right now, keep on keeping on, my friend. Seek your truth, heal your heart, keep your priorities front and center. Know that today and every day, all things come from within oneself. Nobody can take your truth from you. You're stronger than your doubts. You have everything you need already there within you. Fine tune your strengths, show grace to your weaknesses, and just live boldly in the beautiful person that you were meant to be. And always leave things in the hands of your creator. Trust in the

245

journey; after all, this journey is uniquely your own. Enjoy the ride and don't forget to smell the roses along the way.

I let my hair down

It blew freely in the wind

With windows rolled down
And a cool breeze on my face
I didn't know where I was heading
But the ride, I wanted to embrace
I wasn't looking back,
I didn't live there anymore.
I was looking straight ahead,
Anticipating what was in store.
With no expectations of what the future would hold,
I set my cares free in the gust
Ready to let my story unfold.
Freely.
Unapologetically.
Authentically.
Trusting that whatever lies ahead was created just for me.
By Krystle J Bailey

Acknowledgements

This book was a work of my heart. Simply writing it fulfilled me in ways I could never adequately put into words. So many hands went into fulfilling my dream and I am so blessed to experience life with all of you.

Above all, I must give thanks to my creator, my Lord and Savior, Jesus Christ. I am nothing without Him and all things through Him. This book would not have been possible without the guidance of my Father in Heaven and all the mornings we have spent together in prayer, through tears of joy, frustration, doubt, and excitement. My God has led every step.

Nick, my husband. Thank you for listening to every crazy idea, every thought, every doubt, and being my sounding board through every step of this process. Thank you for believing in me from the very beginning and breathing life into my dreams. To Elliana: Thank you for simply being you. Your mere existence changed me and inspires me in new ways every day. To Maceo: Thank you for your wild, crazy, adventurous love. You gave me a deeper sense of purpose and drive when you came into my life.

Thank you, Mom. You showed me how to love from the depths of my soul. You taught me what unconditional love was made of. You believed in me from my first steps and encouraged my love of writing and creation from the earliest stages of my life. Thank you for always being my backbone.

Thank you, Daddy. Thank you for being my guardian angel in Heaven. Thank you for encouraging me and believing in me always. I hope I am making you proud! See you on the other side one day. I love you.

To my stepparents—John and Cheryl. Thank you for selflessly loving me like your own. Thank you for support, encouragement, love, and support every day of my life.

To my sisters both by blood and by love, thank you. Lexi, Tamara, Tierra, Lauren, Morgan, Tara I love you all so much. Thank you for loving me for me and always being a strong shoulder to lean on. You all make me better every day!

A huge thank you to everyone who supported the grassroots growth of *Nourish*. To those who contributed in the early stages and helped bring my dream to life. A special thank you to: Lindsay Lombardi, Yvette Pina, Dana Marino, Rachelle Brown, Jennifer McMahon, Maria Fama, Stephanie Birdsong,

Anita Johnson, Megan Pambianco, Andrea and Jimmy Rovaggi, Morgan Collins, Bethany Stewart, Amanda J Sehee, Jaime Fenn, Cheryl Bassett Morgan, Lauren Richmond, Liz Falciani and Tara Drennen.

To Gaynete Edwards: Thank you for your belief in me and your guidance through this process.

To JimWiz: Your mentorship has meant the world to me! Thank you for being there for every late night, early morning question, doubt, fear, lightbulb, you name it. In the midst of your own creative work and crazy life, you made the time to guide me and believe in me. Thank you! SamWizzy, thank you for sharing your family with me!

Countless other people have contributed to the birth of this book. You all mean so much to me and it is an honor to do life with so many incredible people!

Last but certainly not least, I want to thank you—the reader. I pray that this book has blessed your life in some way. Thank you for taking the time to hear

my heart. God bless you.

About the Author

Krystle J Bailey is a proud wife and mother of two, a wellness coach, business mentor, blogger, social media public figure, and motivational speaker. With a lifelong love of writing, Krystle is bringing her dream of writing to life in her first publication, *Nourish*.

Her daily work involves motivating women on a personal level, helping them to live well in every area of their life from their fitness journey to their spiritual journey. She prides herself on using her God given voice to speak love, light, and positivity into the lives of others. Krystle uses her connections to other women to create communities where every woman has the opportunity to thrive and grow into who she was created to be, to seek her most authentic self, and to begin living boldly in her truth.